BEYOND THE
EXTRAORDINARY

Stories of Modern Day Miracles

BEYOND THE EXTRAORDINARY

Stories of Modern Day Miracles

CRAIG PEARCY

Craig Pearcy
PO Bo 879384
Wasilla, Alaska 99687

HODOS PUBLISHING
480 VERNON, GATINEAU (QUEBEC) CANADA J9J 3K5
613-791-8552

Cover and interior design: Eric Pechin, heaven-design.fr
Photo by Zoltan tasi Okhu rgbjzo on Unsplash

ISBN: 978-2-924586-50-1 (print)
ISBN: 978-2-924586-51-8 (digital)

Legal deposit - Bibliothèque et Archives nationales du Québec, 2021.
Printed in the United States of America.

CONTENTS

ACKNOWLEDGMENTS

Jesus
Ruthie Pearcy
Risa Pearcy
Calin Pearcy
Bob and Sharon Vinson
Charles R. Pearcy
Bill Dew
Carol Dew
Maria Assunção
Alain Caron
Eric Pechin
Sylvia Athey

FOREWORD

What kind of lifestyle should we have as Christians? I know, that's a loaded question, potentially disruptive to our comfort zone. It might challenge some of our deep-rooted habits. But before you freeze and start thinking defensively, hear this: It's all joy!

That's what you will meet in this book: The sheer joy of walking with Jesus on a daily basis and seeing Him touch people's lives with His love and miracles, all through a guy who simply decided not to resist the leading of the Holy Spirit when he meets people.

Craig exudes joy and enters the supernatural with the abandonment and passion of a child. And he is such a storyteller!

It had been a long time since I had read a book that rocked me like this one. I am a Christian author, and I do read Christian books. But to be honest, sometimes I feel like we have to go through many pages before we unearth a few nuggets. It is not so with this book!

Craig's life is literally filled with continual adventures as he opens his mouth, testifies of Jesus, and prays for people.

Yes, on mission trips, yes, in church services, but also on the job as a plumbing contractor, at the store, at the restaurant, on the side of the road, on phone calls, and on and on. It just keeps happening! People start weeping, giving their hearts to Jesus, and receiving healing for all sorts of diseases and conditions. Some start manifesting as demons leave them, and others get filled with the Holy Spirit. Some fall to the ground, overwhelmed by the power of God, right there in a line at the bank, by a restaurant table, or in a basement.

I opened with this question: *What kind of lifestyle should we have as Christians?* We all know the basics: read your Bible and pray every day, go to church on Sunday, be kind to people you meet, and let your light shine. Yet, I'm sure you would agree with me that deep down we often find ourselves longing for more.

Remember the early days when you got to know Jesus? Is it just time passing, or are you settling down into the routines of life? Where did the fire go? No matter what happened, here's some good news: It's not hard at all to get the fire back and burning even brighter.

Craig's going to help us with it.

It's nothing fancy and complicated, nothing anybody can't do. As you read Craig's stories, you'll become convinced that you can do the same and experience the lifestyle you've seen in the book of Acts or in the biographies of great people of faith like Smith Wigglesworth.

Seriously.

Regardless of what we have been experiencing, or not, as a lifestyle, the gospel has not lost its power. It still saves, heals, and sets free. Miracles are definitely still happening today in all types of meetings: in homes, at local churches, in marketplaces, and in stadiums. This is what Craig has discovered. This is what you're about to discover.

So, follow him as he tells how he's just trying to obey what he hears from the Holy Spirit, and your whole perspective on what it means to be a Christian will be renewed and refreshed. I pray a whole new company of believers will be mobilized and sent in the world with the love and passion Craig demonstrates. In this way, we will see a saints movement make a difference and change the nations.

Alain Caron
Apostolic Leader, Hodos Network, Canada
Author of *Apostolic Centers, Apostolic Expansion*
and *The Glory of the Secret Place*

FOREWORD

I met Craig and his wife, Ruthie, in December 2007 while my wife, Carol, and I led a trip to Brazil for Randy Clark's ministry, Global Awakening. We spent the first six days in Taguatinga, a suburb of Brasilia, before flying down to São Paulo to meet up with Randy and have him take over the meetings in a large city nearby, Ribeirão Preto.

What struck me first about Craig was that he was like a gentle bear, but very hungry spiritually. I noticed that he not only engaged in praying for the hundreds that were coming to the twice-a-day meetings, like the other twenty-three team members, but he also followed me at times, shooting video of me ministering. What I didn't know was that this was all relatively new for him, and he was soaking it up like a sponge—and starting to walk into a new anointing.

We all knew something was different when we boarded the plane for the flight down to São Paulo. Everyone turned right to find their seats, but Craig turned left into the open cockpit door. I was thinking, "I know this is Brazil, and they do things a little differently down here, but this can't be legal." Shortly afterward, Craig came out and found his seat, but just before we took off, he returned to the cockpit.

And they let him! He had heard the Lord tell him to go back up there.

We kept waiting for him to come back out. As the flight was approaching the landing and the captain was finishing his announcements, he added, "And, we'd like to welcome the team from Global Awakening to São Paulo." Craig had spent the entire flight in the cockpit, answering the many questions the pilots had for him after they had listened to Craig's stories of what he had just seen and done in Brasilia. As a result, he led them to the Lord, and he was able to give information to the pilot, who had a special needs daughter, about other trips Randy would be making to Brazil so he could get his daughter to a meeting. A true evangelist was born.

This is a book of stories about what Craig has seen and done in the short time he has been out ministering—in foreign countries and right in his hometown while doing his job.

He is not a polished speaker or writer, but his stories remind me of what we read about Smith Wigglesworth, also a plumber. Craig shows us what God can do *to* and *through* someone who simply says yes when God speaks. My wife and I were privileged to speak into Craig's life, encouraging him and seeing him blossom into a powerful little 'ole me (a phrase Randy Clark uses) and be *filled to spill, armed, and dangerous 24/7* (which is something I like to say).

Enjoy this collection of stories, grab hold of the promise of scripture—When the Holy Spirit comes upon you, you will be changed into a different person (see 1 Sam. 10:6)— and say *yes* to what God has for *you*! Craig did!

Bill Dew
Dewnamis Ministries
San Diego, California

In loving memory of our friend Carol Dew,
woman of God .

INTRODUCTION

Hi, the name is Craig Pearcy. Plumber by trade, I'm now fixing more broken hearts and sick bodies than clogged pipes and hot water tanks. This book may sound narcissistic, probably because I'm not sure how to tell these testimonies without including me, being that I was there for all of them. But really, it is a story about God and what He can do through anyone.

I would like simply to start by helping you hit on the desires I believe God has for you. My hope is this: that God will bless you with the knowledge of His wealth and enable you to enjoy His inheritance through experiences of walking with Him. You will be more in love with Jesus, seeing the glorious light of the gospel of Jesus as He reveals the true nature of the Father. May God receive all the glory.

For all of the people who are part of the testimonies in this book—I know God has created you so that you would believe, living a power-filled relationship with God, and shine with the love of Jesus everywhere *as you go*.

My intention in writing this book is that you will experience more of God while reading it, that you will receive a supernatural impartation from the Holy Spirit for boldness, and that it will leave you encouraged and more equipped. Having been washed by the blood, you do not walk alone, but with a helper, the Holy Spirit.

And I will ask the Father, and he will give you another advocate to help you and be with you forever (John 14:16).

But whoever is united with the Lord is one with him in spirit (1 Corinthians 6:17).

Do you not know that your bodies are temples of the Holy Spirit, who is in you, whom you have received from God? You are not your own (1 Corinthians 6:19).

Immediately after so many of these amazing local or global God encounters, ministering the gospel, I would find myself back where I started, like the apostle Paul, a tent maker. I remember on one such occasion—after seeing a great number of people decide to begin following Christ, weeks on end, several times a day, and watching God drop incredible miracles on their lives—I found myself again a plumber, back in some nasty, icky, cold crawl space "gratefully" making a living for my family. Bless God. With spider webs in my hair and water spraying in my face, I worked to repair a broken water line. I remember this exact moment in time so clearly. I had a rock sticking into my knee, causing pain, while remembering that only two days before I had been standing on a big stage in some distant and mysterious land watching God demonstrate His extravagant love and power. *Now I'm here in Alaska, cold and wet?* I thought to myself.

I would continue to repeat this behavior, traveling the world and ministering at least three months out of each year. Yet when back at home, I would do my best to minister however possible to the one in front of me, wherever I was. This naturally caused me to have opportunities to demonstrate God's love and power to my customers.

Some of you might be thinking, *He preached the gospel to his customers?* I will tell you how I did it and how it got easier for me later on in this book. The secret is this: People are not my source and supply; God is. I learned to trust Him more than to settle for the lies of fear of loss or lack. Never be so sure of what you want that you won't settle for something better.

I'm not bold; I did not start out bold. I do not have some natural ability that makes it easy for me to talk with people. My personality is commonly referred to as *introvert*, meaning that I'm OK being by myself. Being an introvert has been, for me, a learned behavior, a coverup for fear, an excuse I developed, a tool to protect myself from the possibility of being rejected by people. As an introvert, I would not be expected to do things that were outside my comfort zone.

Thank God I could not do these things on my own. I recognized my need for the Holy Spirit. That is when I began a greater level of commitment to saying *no* to the world and *yes* to Jesus. That is when I allowed myself to begin to encounter Christ and see the glorious light of the gospel more clearly.

> *The god of this age has blinded the minds of unbelievers, so that they cannot see the light of the gospel that displays the glory of Christ, who is the image of God* (2 Corinthians 4:4).

Still, at the age of 39, my comfort zone included going through the motions on cruise control, doing my time, just doing life, which included sitting in church on Sunday earning points for heaven. Even though I might have told you I was born again, I was just faking it. The world hadn't yet experienced who God had designed me to be. I hadn't changed very much in my life, other than being set free from drugs and alcohol. Thank You, Jesus!

Finally, realizing that this mediocre, lukewarm lifestyle was just not enough, I gave it up. I decided to quit lukewarm. I repented, asking God to forgive me for letting fear control my life and for not trusting Him. That's when I began to say, "Yes, God, I'm in," and, "God, I trust You with my everything!" Before that, it was just me thinking, *I'm in; I'm saved.* It was just me thinking about me.

Now my focus began to change. The new me was shoving all my chips into the center of the table: "Take me; I'm yours!" That was the beginning of everything you'll read in this book.

> *And we all, who with unveiled faces contemplate the Lord's glory, are being transformed into his image with ever-increasing glory, which comes from the Lord, who is the Spirit* (2 Corinthians 3:18).

The testimonies in this book are of God's grace; His son, Jesus; and His love and power. The stories in the following chapters are a product of the love of Jesus expressed through me. They happened through Him, who loved me first, before I ever loved Him. As Philippians 4:13 says, *"I can do all this through him who gives me strength."*

The encounters in this book were, for me, many times a deep personal act of sacrificial worship, a response to His love for me. In these times of worship, He has allowed me to make a sacrifice of myself by making the first step, pushing past the fear in order to relay the love of Jesus. It has always been the hardest thing for me to make the first move.

Through him then let us continually offer up a sacrifice of praise to God, that is, the fruit of lips that acknowledge his name. Do not neglect to do good and to share what you have, for such sacrifices are pleasing to God (Hebrews 13:15–16 ESV).

People refer to me as an evangelist. I like to say that I'm just a follower of Jesus who refuses to keep my mouth shut.

Even though I was being trained daily, years would pass by before I began to notice that I had been equipped intentionally by God to do the works of service. Early on, I had no idea I was being tuned up for something more. From pure hunger, I would simply go to every conference and training session that I could in order to get more of Jesus. In this process, without having a practical trainer who could show me how to preach the gospel or heal the sick, I learned to hear God's voice, preach the gospel, heal the sick, and cast out demons. I began learning to do the practical part of the gospel to reach the lost on my own with Holy Spirit as my helper.

One Sunday morning in 2007, one of my in-the-box prophetic teachers stopped me before the Sunday service and told me how proud he was of how I was continually reaching the lost and healing the sick.

I thanked him and replied, "I'm just doing what everyone else is doing."

He gave me the strangest look and said, "There is barely a person in this church who lives this like you do!"

The Holy Spirit encouraged me with this statement and also helped me see an opportunity to help others follow Jesus, accept the gifts of the Holy Spirit, and do the stuff. Maybe this book will be part of that.

May God bless you as you read this book. I pray you will live freely, extravagantly loving God and loving people *as you go*. My prayer is that you will experience more of God while reading this book and that you will receive an impartation for boldness that will leave you encouraged, connected to the body of Jesus Christ and the truth of the gospel, and more equipped to do the works of service.

Having been washed by the blood, you are walking not alone, but with the Holy Spirit.

—Craig Pearcy

Chapter 1
IN MY LIFE

It was September 13, 1992, in Paso, Washington. Hearing an altar call, I found myself running down a church aisle, sliding to the altar on my knees, and making the most wonderful and difficult decision of my life. At 29 years of age, I said yes to Jesus.

As I ran down the aisle toward the pastor standing on the platform, I felt someone grab my shirt collar. I stopped and looked back, thinking it was maybe the man who had invited me, but nobody was there. Then I heard the words, "I'm the world, and if you do this, you will give up everything." The world was literally trying to pull me back! I remembered all that the world had offered me, and I determinedly said, "I'm giving my life to Jesus!"

The next memory I have is of kneeling at the altar with tears streaming down my face. I got to my feet after praying with the pastor, and I could feel, physically, that I had really changed. Something had taken place, and I knew I was glowing with this new light shining inside of me. Nothing seemed the same, and I knew that the glow within me would be visible to everyone who looked at me. I was actually so sure of this that I felt self- conscious and really wondered if people could see it.

Returning home that afternoon, I said to God, "If You are real and that experience was real, please could You take away my addiction?" The next day, I realized that I had given over to Jesus the very thing I thought I would forever have to battle—the craving for drugs and alcohol. I was free! When I handed myself over to God, I realized that I *did* believe and was now close to a true love who had died to set me free.

Yes, He made a way for me when He rose again—and I rose again, too, filled with Him, after dying to myself. This experience, and many others that I treasure, can never be taken away. I live in an ongoing Daddy experience, and He's mad about me. He perceives me through eyes filled with love, and when I look at Him, I get lost in His eyes. Thank You, Jesus! I'm not afraid anymore.

Desires Fulfilled

My wife, Ruthie, and I were talking and dreaming about making a road trip in the lower forty-eight states. We have several places we would like to visit. One morning, Ruthie and I were in our prayer room. After praying, Ruthie said that if we would be making road trips, we would need a car that gave us good mileage. That night, as I was about to fall asleep, I contemplated what she had said about needing a car. We were not really car people. In fact, in all our married years, we had never owned a car, but always trucks. I remember I said to God, "If she wants a car, then OK, give her a car."

The next day, I was looking at a potential job for our plumbing company, and while doing so, I managed to help a customer save a lot of money on his project. As the customer and I continued to discuss the project, we were walking through his garage, and parked in one of the bays was a 2,000 Cadillac Deville. As I passed the car, I said, "I just saved you lots of money—give me that car!"

Lo and behold, as soon as I made the request, he replied, "Done!" Bless You, Jesus, for answering a simple request of the heart!

Financial Miracle—June 2016

I try to be thankful for everything, acknowledging everything God does, but I still don't have a real understanding of all He does on my behalf. One time, while in Columbia for the second of three trips in 2016, as I waited for my flight to depart from Cali Airport, I sat in my seat and began to acknowledge God. I began to be thankful for all He had done again on this most recent ministry trip—all the signs, miracles, wonders, and salvations.

Then I began asking God for a real financial miracle, like the ones I had heard of so many times, when God would do amazing things financially in people's lives—paying off debts or sending money from an unknown source. My request was somewhere between a simple prayer and a thought.

While these thoughts and prayers were taking place, I realized that I was actually sitting in a similar location on the plane, and on the same tarmac, as I had been when God gave me my call to ministry years before. This call came even before I knew a person could have such an encounter with God.

I remember, for just the slightest moment, thinking selfishly that since I had given so much of my time and finances, been away from my family so much over the years, and had been doing my part and not counting the cost, that I would also like to personally experience a really big financial miracle. And I was at the same time reminding myself that no matter what, I would remain unshakable in pressing forward with the gospel of Jesus Christ. I was thinking these thoughts while the plane began to taxi to the runway.

A few days after I arrived back home in Alaska, my wife and I were moving forward with our plans to downsize and get a smaller house so that we would be out of debt and better able to travel and preach the gospel.

We met with our realtor, who was helping us list our house, in which we had raised our family and had lived for the last twenty-three years. As we talked with this man, he began to ask us what our plans were—where we were going to live after our house was sold and why we were selling. We explained that we were selling to get ourselves in better financial shape so I could travel more to minister.

The realtor asked where we were going to live, and I said we were going to downsize and buy this little house overlooking the airport. He said, "What do you really want?" I immediately blurted out my answer, which caused him to sit back in his chair and look at me like I had lost my mind. I explained to him all that we wanted in a house, and he politely told me, "For you to have a house like you just described, that would be God! You just don't have the equity."

Two days later, after church, my wife and I went to lunch with another couple. The husband had, a few years ago, gone on a mission trip with me to the Philippines. The four of us had begun to build a relationship from that point.

They had become great friends to us and had donated money and time to the ministry.

Over lunch, during the course of conversation, we told these friends that we wanted to sell our house so that we would be in better financial shape and be free to minister.

They asked us where we were going to live. We told them that after we sold our house, we would have enough money to buy a very small house and be out of debt, and that would be about it. Then this man asked me, "What do you really want?" I answered the same way I had with the realtor, explaining what I wanted in a house.

Their expressions changed as I described the home we would really like to have, and they looked at each other and then back at us. Then they said, "We have a house on our property that is exactly like you described, and we have no idea what to do with it. Would you like to see it?"

Within the hour, we were at the property, and it had everything we had hoped for—the view, the exact size, and the layout. It was so amazing to see this place, because it was everything we wanted. The problem facing us was that in the natural we could not afford to buy something like that while also having the money necessary to make the needed construction improvements. It was very hard for us to see something so close to what we wanted and not be able to have it.

The next day, a Monday, at 11:00 am, I received a phone call from this friend who owned the property, and he said, "My wife and I would like to let you finish the property to your standards and live there as long as you like. When you don't want to live there anymore, we will give you back all the money you put into the property. You can live there rent free with no taxes!"

Within a few days, we were working on the property, making the construction improvements. As we began finishing the property, I found myself traveling back to Cali, Colombia, for the third time that year—back to where I had asked for a financial miracle. Over the next week, as I ministered, I saw God do so much in the lives of so many, and I was again really astounded by His goodness.

When I returned home to Alaska, my wife and I were invited over to the same friends' house for lunch. The conversation quickly turned to the property, and again we were overcome by God's love. Here is what they told us during lunch: "We have decided to subdivide the land we own here, donating that portion of the land and the house to your ministry!" God, we're so thankful! Thank you, Hendricksons!

Another time, our home, which we had had listed for sale for over a year, had its first showing, and we got an offer. By the end of the following month, we had closed on the home. Ruthie and I had told each other that when we had the credit cards paid off and the money saved, we would go on a vacation to Hawaii. Now, with the house sold and the credit cards paid off, I got a call from an old friend who was a YWAM director in Kona, Hawaii. He invited Ruthie and me to come and "just be me" with their students. The offer included airfare and accommodations. I quickly agreed. We spent the next nine months in Kona, where God taught me how to be discipled and how to disciple. Jesus, we bless You!

They Let Me

I spend a lot of my time away from my family at great risk, utilizing my own personal financial resources to go to various countries around the world to preach the gospel, disciple people, and heal the sick. It's not easy to describe exactly how I spend several months of each year, or even to explain the reason for it all. Yet it's my current reality.

Many of the local people I meet, who encounter God through little ole me, end up getting healed and maybe believing with their hearts or receiving prophetic words from God *as I go*. These divine appointments, which I ask God for, happen several times a day as I have the opportunity to talk with people about my Jesus.

It's so simple and refreshing. These people I meet on the street *let me talk with them!* Even with an audience of just one or two, here in Alaska, I talk with them, feeding them truth *because they let me!* Feeding the hunger with love is the key. People are so hungry for something real, and usually these people are unknowingly desperate for the love of the Father. This is fantastic training for the global *as I go*.

I have been asked, "Why do you rarely share the testimonies of signs, miracles, and wonders from your times ministering in Brazil, Colombia, Philippines, Argentina, and other countries all over the globe?" The answer is this: My *as I go* is different from yours. I would not want to cause people to think for a second that they have to be some sort of traveling minister with credentials, or an apostolic leader who goes to exotic places, in order to be a part of what God is doing.

I will say this: I was entrusted with one breath of air. God watched what I did with that gift, and then He said, "Craig, you did that pretty well." With that, God gave me another breath and another. Gifts are given to good stewards. I'm not among the most talented. I'm not someone who can memorize the most Scripture, nor am I well spoken. I am just willing. I am one of those who hear the word and then do the word. God saw that I was obedient and able to be entrusted with the one in front of me in my tiny town of Wasilla, Alaska, so He expanded my territory.

Being an itinerant minister of the gospel of Jesus has not changed the responsibility I have for the one in front of me. I must admit, I have had that thought: *Because I minister globally to many people, doing all that for God, maybe I'm exempt from loving as I go locally.* That thought was poison and had to be quickly and continuously dismissed. If I don't reach the lost *as I go* at home, in the work place, or in Walmart, I know I have no business thinking I have something to export. What am I exporting?

If I don't do the stuff at home, if it's not my normal life to live a naturally supernatural lifestyle at home, then I have nothing to talk about when going overseas. Without living a supernatural lifestyle at home, I have no business and nothing to give away or impart when I'm away from Alaska. The testimony of Jesus in my life has been my battle flag, and it's what has caused glorious success in my travels. Bless Jesus!

Do you want to know how to minister the gospel? Make it your life. First, seek the Kingdom. Get past whatever is holding you back by moving toward the fear and realizing that the fear is not real. I should say that again: Go toward the fear.

Let me tell you right now—you get ready by doing, by getting out there and trying, by getting knocked down and getting back up and then trying again. If I listened to every religious goofball who told me I wasn't ready to minister, thousands of people may not have entered the Kingdom. Thousands may not have experienced His power for salvation. And so many would have missed out on experiencing God demonstrating His love. You don't have to fit the mold of how others want you to minister. Believe me, just be yourself and listen to God.

All people know is: I'm a simple guy with a clunky message; people get healed, saved and delivered; and I have been with Jesus. It's all about ministering as you go. So go! Recently, as I was about to fly again to South America, God said to me, "Preach the gospel like it's your last hour on earth, like what you say in that hour will determine whether you will spend eternity in heaven or hell."

Chapter 2
HIS WORD

I can tell you about a time when I would hear a voice but didn't know whose it was. I think, if you were to ask me, I would not even have known who I was obeying. My first real recollection of someone communicating with me was probably in the fall of 1984. I had a dream that was so vivid that, to this day, I still remember exactly what happened in it and what followed in the natural.

In the dream, I was downhill skiing in an area near the city that I lived in at the time. It was the most beautiful day in my dream, and as I skied, I saw before me a large snow drift some way down the slope. I had skied on that slope so often over the years, and in the natural I had never seen anything like what I was seeing in my dream—in which I skied down the hill, hit a snow drift/jump, and was tossed into the air. While high above the jump, and still in midair, I looked around and admired the beauty of my surroundings without any fear of falling to the hard, packed snow.

Not long after the dream, I was skiing with my buddies when I saw this large snowdrift that had never been in that particular place before. At that point, I had not yet recalled the dream. I hit the snowdrift, went up much higher than I would ever have wanted to, and at that moment, I recalled the dream as it flowed into the natural in exactly the same way.

Just as I had in my dream, I could look around at the beauty of my surroundings, and I could even see my friends who didn't hit the jump standing by and watching me in the air. I don't know how high I went into the air, and when I hit the ground, the snow was as solid as a rock. But I felt no pain, and I didn't hurt myself. Thinking I was hurt, people began to come up the hill. They found me sitting there, stunned, with my skis off. At that moment I couldn't quite process what had just taken place. The thought of God never passed through my mind. I knew I had been forewarned somehow, yet I never tried to make sense of the event.

Months later, in the summer of 1985, I had another dream that brought me to a higher level of realization. I was to end a relationship, and I did it obediently and quickly—still not questioning who or why, but just obeying the dream. I continued to obey, but now I knew this: I must be obedient to the voice, and believe me (as simple as it sounds), I did what I was told. By that time, I was driving by churches and contemplating attending one. I recall one Sunday when I drove past a few and realized that I was being intentionally drawn to them.

My first real example of simple obedience to this voice was on December 31, 1985, at 11:55 pm. I was at a New Year's Eve party with a date, just celebrating the occasion with friends, when I heard a voice telling me to go to a particular bar in the locality. I was sober, and I headed for the door, thinking I ought to inform my date that I was leaving, but not doing so.

I found myself in my truck, headed to a local watering hole, and I had no idea why. When I arrived, I walked up to the only person I knew (we'll call him Terry), all the while wondering why I was even in that place. Then suddenly I saw a girl standing against the back wall. She was absolutely beautiful, and I was completely taken by her.

I told my friend standing next to me, "See that girl? I'm going to marry her."

He looked at me and said, "Shut up!" Six months later, we were married.

Later on, I heard His voice again, but this time I was full on disobedient to that voice. I'm certain that this caused me to enter the desert—a time of not hearing His voice. It was clear I had no intentions of obeying. I don't recall hearing His voice again until years later, when I said yes to going to church with a friend. I obeyed His voice and went back the next Sunday.

His Voice Is Key

After my salvation experience, I really did not hear the voice like I had known it before—sort of aloud, if you will. It was compelling, but not demanding. It was a voice that drew me, a voice that my heart recognized even before I knew it was God.

Once again, I experienced another dream, years later, while not fully following God. As I was saved, I had a radical life change, but didn't know what to do with that experience, having just moved back to Alaska.

Occasionally we would visit a church, but we never put down roots. This next dream caused me to realize that I was to come to the cross for both myself and my wife. Again, disobedient, I didn't follow through, and a few more years went by as I drifted through various churches, judging them all based on who was in the service, the money talk, the "crazy" worship, and various people and things I couldn't connect with.

Eventually, many things contributed to the decision to connect with a church. One was my wife telling me, with the kids in tow, "We're going to church. Are you going with us?"

I heard the voice again, like in the old days, "Are you going to become the man I created you to be, or are you going to sit on the couch on Sundays and be a NASCAR daddy?"

I thought for an instant and replied, "I'm going with you."

I walked into the church, and I heard the voice again, knowing it was God. He said, "Keep your eyes on me." I felt like He gave me blinders, which gave me a safe spot to be in His presence and not even know who was in the room or have to watch the congregation jump around.

Months went by before I would even look to see who was speaking on the stage. I began to have encounters with God and hear His voice during the church services. I heard Him, in worship one Sunday, say, "Look at all these people." I began to look around at all the people in church as they worshipped. Then He said, "Get to know them." That's another story, but I did just that.

As I grew and got to know the people, I learned to forgive. I also had other opportunities to be equipped, not even knowing that could happen. For instance, I attended a

Saturday meeting where a guest speaker came to our church and spoke on hearing God's voice. To me, this was really interesting, as I did not know that a person could hear more often than just once in a while. During that meeting, I heard God tell me what He had named me. He had given me a name other than Craig. When I heard the name, I asked Him to spell it, and He did—Protha.

As I grew, I began to seek God and talk to God, if only in my mind. I prayed a lot, but hardly ever out loud, unless it was for a person or in a situation where it was expected to be out loud.

I continued to learn to be obedient and move in the direction of His voice, not needing to hear His voice really loudly anymore, but obeying on the slightest whisper and then heeding what I believed He had trained me for—His purpose. Thus, I was anticipating what He might require me to do as I understand His heart for people.

I had a fellow minister once say to me, "I don't know anyone who can hear God's voice like you do." My explanation is that it's easier to hear the Father's voice when your heart is set to be obedient.

Respond to what He *may* say before He has said it. I make the first move with His heart; He always meets me in that place and speaks through me. He got my attention by speaking to me, and now He speaks through me, and I begin to understand the Commander's will that none should perish.

With God constantly on the move, I try to not go where He has been, but to go where He is going to be. I hear His voice from a place of obedience. I act on what He shows me, but more importantly, I act on what He has already shown me—that none should perish. God has taught me to hear

His voice and also to know His ways. Many times, I move on what He might say or that He may say something. I have tried myself to move on the slightest whisper or on the fact that a whisper may come. I understand the Commander's intent. And it's when I move in faith and obedience that I am met with more—when I need it to do His will.

Knowledge

Lots of people teach on what's referred to as *words of knowledge* (see 1 Corinthians 12). I might like to expand on that. Knowledge is a gift. It's what you know, and it's having tapped into the realm that carries this information. It's learning to tap in and discern what information is of heaven and who it's for and to believe for His word to manifest itself.

He allows the knowledge gate to open as He determines, and you need to be standing by the gate, asking the right questions, when it happens.

Chapter 3
AS I RIDE

Driving the Alcan Highway

I did it! Marysville, Washington, to Wasilla, Alaska. I had successfully completed what we Alaskans call "Driving the Alcan Highway." If you do this in a car, it's really just a lot of driving. I've done it eight times over the years.

On a bike, it's a whole different experience, as I learned firsthand. Here are a few of the lessons I discovered:

#1. Screeching to a halt, I realized I had made a little mistake. I was on a motorcycle in the middle of a Bison herd. Quickly assessing my situation, I noticed another tourist in a motorhome who had stopped opposite the herd with his camera pointed at me. He was taking a video of me, probably hoping to make the next YouTube sensation.

Those guys had a motorhome. I was on a bike. Fear and impending doom overcame me as a very large, horned death machine, only ten feet away, communicated with me without words. I could read in his eyes, "Tiny white man, I will end you if you rev that motor one more time!"

At that point, I began asking Jesus if that was really how it was going to end for me—found dead along the Alcan Highway, clutching a smashed iPhone, next to a hoof-dented Yamaha.

#2. I learned that some motorcycle-riding, leather-clad men of the highway don't perform the standard wave at other motorcyclists who wear safety-green neon coats. Others don't wave at those who don't know how to properly wave at other passing motorcyclists who are wearing safety-green neon coats.

#3. I didn't follow the driving directions from the overly friendly group of Hell's Angels, and I respectfully declined their offer to go to a party that night. I convinced myself that Jesus would not have gone with them either.

#4. I have found that most adventure riders are very friendly and that some would be fine extras in a Mad Max sequel. While at least two others were as dumb as me, riding north toward a snow storm on the Alaska border. At least I would be easy to find in the spring in my safety-green neon coat!

#5. During my last night in a tent, I rediscovered the sound a black bear makes when he is sniffing around a camp site at night—as I lay in my tent in deep intercessory emergency prayer while resembling a plump bear burrito smothered in waterproof nylon.

#6. I learned that the smell of adrenaline-tainted urine filtered through a $400 sleeping bag will not drive bears away from a camp site.

#7. I will pay $135 for a hotel room. (See #5 and #6.)

#8. I will drive 900 miles in one day. (See #5, #6, and #7.)

#9. When you pass a vehicle that looks like it might belong to the Canadian Mounted Police, and out of the corner of your eye you notice that you are wearing matching safety-green neon coats, do not speed up after the pass to 135K (82 MPH).

#10. I saw other riders in safety-green neon coats. They waved.

#11. No one waves at riders who are wearing mittens. Or red sparkly helmets with 1972 bubble wind screens.

On this trip cruising through Canada, I had several opportunities to talk with people about my Jesus. I have found that this type of motorcycle is a real conversation starter.

I had the nicest time sharing my testimony at a hot spring resort in Canada with a married British couple who seemed very interested and engaged in every word about how my life changed after I gave it to Jesus. This experience was really wonderful. I could definitely tell they were seeking a better life. That could very well have been what their motorcycle trip was all about.

Healing on the Highway

About to leave San Diego, California, heading for Phoenix Arizona, I stopped at a busy gas station to fuel up my bike. I stepped between the bike and the pump, and the next thing I knew, my motorcycle fell over onto me, trapping me against the fuel pump. I was pinned against the pump, with the weight of the bike and all my gear on me, being crushed and feeling ridiculous and helpless. I looked around, hoping someone would come to my aid. I yelled for help, still believing a Good Samaritan would rush to my assistance, when I realized that I was adorned in safety yellow clothing and very much invisible in California. I was on my own.

I managed to push the bike partially off of myself, using all of my strength, when it started to roll slightly away from me. Trying to avoid another disaster, I made an awkward move and pulled almost all the muscles in my left leg and on the left side of my back. I was instantly in extreme pain, yet I held on to the bike and was able to get it into gear so that it didn't roll any farther. When I finally got the bike up and resting on its kickstand, I realized I was badly hurt.

After some time, I was able to get onto the bike and ride to a place where I could stop and collect myself. As I pulled over in a mall parking lot and got off the bike, a friendly stranger walked past, and we began to chat about my bike and my Alaska license plates. We chatted for a moment, and then I asked him, "Are you a Christian?"

He hesitated, appearing to consider the question, and then replied, "Yes, I am."

He told me that he went to a local church. I told him I was in pain and asked if he would pray for me. Again he hesitated, as if it had never crossed his mind to do such a thing, and he looked at me in a surprised way, as if to say, "Oh you want me to pray for you now!" After a moment he began to pray something like, "Oh God, you're a good God." As he fumbled for words, I thought to myself that it was truly wonderful that this guy who had probably never ever prayed for anyone was praying for me—and I was so happy for him. I was his first. This made me really happy, and I thanked him profusely for the prayer. However, I was still in a lot of pain. I got back on the bike and rode for a few hours, but soon I realized I just had to pull over and get off of this motorcycle.

As the pain continued to escalate, I finally pulled over at a viewpoint parking area next to the freeway and tried to stretch my leg and back muscles so that I could keep riding. Just then, a big rig pulled up and a truck driver and her dog jumped out of the truck. The dog immediately ran up to me very happily, and when the woman came after her dog, I asked her, "Are you a Christian?" And very similar to the guy in San Diego, the woman prayed for me. I was really grateful, especially as I realized that I was unintentionally equipping the saints to do the work of ministry—healing the sick! All at once, the pain was gone, and I was healed for real!

I didn't realize it while the woman prayed, but when I attempted to get back on my bike, I noticed the pain had completely gone! Bless God! I was so excited that I couldn't wait to get to my dad's house in Arizona to tell him all about how I got healed! However, upon arriving at his home, where I was going to stay for a few days, I realized I had a large infection on my arm. It was red, and the skin was hot. I just prayed it wasn't serious.

After telling my dad the amazing story of how I got healed, I asked him to pray for me. Once again, I was his first. I don't think he had ever done anything like that before. I encouraged him to just pray the words that came to his mind, so he prayed, and immediately the infection was healed on the spot! All the redness was gone, and the area where the infection had been was now actually cold to the touch—very noticeably so! As we felt around the area that had been infected not so long before, we were both so amazed and excited about what God had just done. I was especially happy that my dad had prayed and witnessed God perform a miracle.

Chapter 4
HEALING AROUND THE WORLD

Fire in Brazil

One night, during our last meeting on a trip to Brazil, Holy Spirit fire (*fogo*, which means "fire" in Portuguese) fell, and we were bombarded with several testimonies of healing and deep heart encounters. (I hadn't even prayed for healing!) One man was healed of a very painful mosquito-related disease. On a Wednesday night, when we were at another church, he found out where we would be that night, and he brought his wife to the meeting. She was also healed of the same illness—from just simply being in God's presence! There were several other testimonies of God healing physical infirmities that night. The following day, I crossed the continent to Cali, Colombia.

Ministering in Cali, Colombia

In Cali, Columbia, worship was amazing. I really love worshipping with these people. My good friend, Gabe

Jonson, led worship, and then I began ministering with words of knowledge, and people were healed. When people were healed, they became a ministry team. I had them go around the room, after I prayed for them, to lay hands on the sick people who would be healed.

Then I did an open call for prayer. A woman came forward very slowly, barely able to walk. I pulled a chair out quickly so that she was able to sit down. After she sat down, I asked her what she wanted prayer for. She said she had an ulcer on her leg. She showed me the bandage around the ulcer and said she did not want to unwrap it, but she was in very much pain. She also mentioned that she almost did not have the strength to come to the meeting, but she forced herself to come, believing that God would heal her. I began to prophesy over her, and the Holy Spirit revealed to me that she was an intercessor. Her actual job title was Chief Intercessor, and the pastor who was standing behind me confirmed these words.

I commanded the pain to leave the woman's body, and then I asked her to stand up. My expectation was that she might say she was feeling much better and then maybe just walk back to her chair. What I did not expect was what happened next: she jumped up, waved her hands around, shouted, and then took off running. She ran to the back of the church and began to run laps around the room. The scene reminded me of an old time Pentecostal meeting. It was very exciting to see this woman totally healed.

Hearing Restored

I was ministering in a new church with a pastor I had never met before. I had barely finished ministering when he said he wanted to take me to a school for the hearing impaired the following day. This pastor seemed happy about how things had gone that night in his church, and when I heard about our plan for the next day, I was excited, because I love to see people experience God. At the same time, however, I felt like the pastor was challenging me and God.

So, off I went to this school for the hearing impaired. I was immediately ushered to the front of the room where about seventy teenagers were waiting, all of them Brazilian. Nobody had told them why I was there, so I started to explain in English, which one person translated into Portuguese, and then another person translated into sign language for these teens.

As I told them that I have prayed for people and that often God has healed them, the teens began pointing to their ears. The leader of the pack, however, sat in the middle of the room, doing her best to distract the others and persuade them not to believe what I was saying. That's when I heard God say, "Pray for her first!"

I proceeded to ask this beautiful young lady to come up front. Causing as much distraction as possible, she came forward, signing that she did not believe any of this, but that I could pray for her anyway. The first two times I prayed, nothing changed. The third time I prayed, praise God, this young girl's ears opened, and she just freaked out. What's more, she became an instant believer, and in a few seconds, she became God's finest helper. She wanted everyone healed, and the place got kind of crazy.

Kids were jumping to their feet, because they all wanted this touch from God. It was so exciting to see God pour out on these young people. Together, the young lady and I kept praying, and she was hearing and speaking the words I said. Wow! That was fantastic! She was speaking the words I said without even needing to watch my lips move so she could read them. So, to prove it again, I stood behind her.

At that point, the other kids were sitting on the edge of their seats as we fully demonstrated that this young girl was healed. She began to invite others forward, and in the next few minutes, a total of six were healed.

While this was taking place, the leadership of this professional school for the hearing impaired burst in and began breaking up the meeting. They had just realized what was actually happening in their school. As I was leaving, I came around the corner and guess what I saw—kids praying for other kids. Two of the kids who had been healed were praying for two others who were being healed. Eight were healed!

Tumor Gone

At the end of the service one night, a mother brought her daughter to me. The little girl had a tumor on her brain and she had stomach problems, both of which were causing her a lot of pain. When I put my hands on her head, I felt a pop under my left hand. I asked if her headache was still there, and looking astonished, she said it wasn't. I put my hand on her stomach for five seconds and then asked if she still had pain. She said she didn't. Jesus, thank You.

The Healed Heal

One Thursday night really surprised me. There was such a great eagerness for the anointing and a release of knowledge in this church, which resulted in physical healing. God was showing me precisely who had pain, what type, and where in their bodies. Some people said they were healed when the word of knowledge was spoken. These folks became that night's ministry team. It was so good to see them pray for others and then see the people they prayed for encounter God.

Miracles in Fortaleza

Every meeting we have held in Fortaleza, we have seen God do many extraordinary miracles—including tumors, lumps, and cysts disappearing. Even the maid in the place where I was staying in the city felt the fire of God in the area where she needed a miracle after we prayed for her.

When we interviewed people at the meetings about the physical healings God has been doing, we have heard mostly about healing of the really painful Chikungunya (a mosquito-borne illness), as well as healing of lumps and tumors.

On a Wednesday night, everyone in the room saw a man with a huge thoracic cavity filled with cancer get healed. Words of knowledge have been really effective as well.

One time, a lady in the middle of the room received a touch from the Lord as her eyesight was restored and pain from Chikungunya was healed. A girl to her right, excited about her friend's miracle, had her leg grow out when I twirled her up from her seat once to the right and then to the left. There were such tears of joy. All this happened as the ministry leader stood by. All he said was, "You have a unique ministry style!" And then he smiled.

During one meeting, a young lady told her mother that her ear pain went away while I was sharing my testimony.

One morning at a Fortaleza Drug Rehab Center, several of the men were healed of various ailments. The important part was that they all agreed that Jesus is the Messiah, and they all wanted to begin following Him.

At an afternoon meeting at a Ladies' Drug Rehab Center, while the ladies were resting in the arms of Jesus, several of them reported that they had been healed. Many experienced incredible miracles, including the disappearance of lumps in their abdomens. A young lady was healed of a constant pain in her abdomen, and her friend was also healed of various pains.

My translator from Brazil called me one day with an incredible testimony of Jesus. A lady who had come to one of the meetings in Fortaleza during my last trip had been totally healed. Her lung had failed, and she had a tumor on the same side. The day after the meeting, she was scheduled to have surgery for the cancer. Instead, the doctor asked her what had happened to the tumor and how her lung was healed. Jesus! I am so thankful for my anointed translator and co-minister, Maria Assunção, in Fortaleza, Brazil, who partners with and conveys heaven.

I have at times felt like I am not meant to say a lot about what has happened in Brazil, or even about the meetings, other than, "Jesus has happened here, and I know what I was created to do!" It turns out that this has required love, practice, patience, and relationships. I'm doing what I love. At one meeting, I encountered God's heart for His kids. This encounter shook me to my core. I could not even talk when it happened. I cried when I tried to speak, and I think I witnessed just a small part of His heart, because I'm still alive to talk about it.

Please hear this: God said *go*. He didn't say, "The most anointed should go." He said He would send us a Helper who is more anointed than the anointed, even more anointed than the self-appointed anointed. So go! It's so easy to compare yourself with someone else and then stay on the sidelines. You will be amazed by how God will use you. So just go!

Full-on Blowout Meeting

I asked four very young girls to be my prayer ministry team one night. They boldly laid hands on the sick, and the people were immediately healed. We saw many people with lumps in their abdomens getting healed.

I know it's hard to believe, but here is a snippet of one of my days in Brazil:

- Children in a poor community school respond to an altar call for salvation.

- I get suited up to go and pray for a man who would come out of his coma later in the day. Doctors and family said they were waiting for him to die.

- During a mass prayer, in which we commanded pain to go, a lady in a floral dress was healed of all sorts of pain in various parts of her body.

- A girl in black had a vision of Jerusalem with Jesus—a wonderful and amazing testimony of seeing Jesus in the meeting.

- I had a word of knowledge, and I pointed at a girl, asking if she had a baby sibling at home with an ear infection. She said she did, and I prayed for her to have an impartation to heal the sick. In the meeting, several people that she prayed for were healed. I am believing she took that impartation home with her.

- I had a word of knowledge for a lady in black and asked if she had pain in a specific spot on her back. She said she did, and moments later, she was healed. The children said she must have told me, but after the next few words of knowledge, they were convinced that God was in the house.

Cancer Healed in Fortaleza

On one particular night, I preached a message called "The Hem of the Robe." When I do this, I encourage people to come forward if they have faith. Sometimes, this is really easy, and people just jump up and run forward. One memorable night, a boy was so anxious to receive his healing that he just jumped up and ran forward, and as he ran, his mother chased him up the aisle. I bent over to stop the child from running into me, as I wasn't sure what he was really doing, and as I turned the palm of my hand towards his belly to halt him, I felt a tumor in his abdomen just under the skin. At that exact moment, I felt the tumor burst. I almost expected to see something manifest under his shirt or drop out onto the floor, but I didn't actually see any of these things.

I told my translator, Maria, what had just happened, and she relayed it to the mother of the boy. The mother checked her son for the tumor, and to her surprise, she found that it had disappeared. Her boy was healed.

But this night, as I was once again preaching on "The Hem of the Robe," I tried to trigger a response by telling stories about how people would jump up and run toward the stage to receive healing. As I did this, a few people came forward, and God healed them. After that, people returned to their seats, and I continued to speak, praising God for healing the people who had come forward.

Then a man stood to his feet. He was very old and feeble. His skin looked gray, and he was very thin. As he stood up, he very slowly raised his head, looked at me, and began walking slowly toward me. I was concerned that he would not even make it. We could tell he was in terrible pain. I also noticed something very unusual—both his chest cavity and abdomen were distended, and it was clear to me, and everyone in the room, that something was very wrong with this man. By the time he reached me, hoping to receive his miracle, the had pastor told me he had invited this man to come to church that night and that he was not a believer. The pastor added that the man was convinced that if he came he would be healed.

Sometimes I feel challenged by people's expectations, and I mistakenly think I have something to do with a person being healed. The truth is, it isn't me who does or doesn't heal someone. It's only the power of God. With this in mind, I had one hand on the man's lower back and one hand on his chest while he faced the gathering of people. I don't remember saying anything. I just remember praying. It's almost like I wasn't even really there, because I didn't really see what the other people were seeing.

Suddenly, there was a gasp from the crowd. People were pointing, and some were standing in an attempt to get a better view of what was happening. I wasn't really aware of what was going on. I didn't understand what the people in the room had seen.

As I looked into the crowd, I could see people with their mouths hanging open, and some were pointing at the man. I decided to step back to see what they were looking at. It was then that I realized the man's stomach was no longer distended, and neither was his chest! His body was back to normal. It was a holy moment.

A few days later, in one of our meetings, we interviewed the man. He told us that all the pain had left his body, and he didn't feel sick anymore. He was healed. I prayed for the man again, covering him with the precious blood of Jesus. I had hoped this would be a grand event and this man would live for many years to come. I found out sometime later that the man died from the cancer, as it had returned.

I would have liked to have seen this man filled with the Spirit of the Lord. But sadly, after he was healed, he stopped seeking the Lord. I'm left with this thought—his room had been cleaned, but not occupied, so the cancer returned and filled the void (see Matt. 12:43–45).

Chapter 5
KIDS ARE THE KEY

My wife, Ruthie, and I were on a ministry trip to Brazil, where we ministered in churches and schools during the day. Usually, after the main speaker preached on healing, our team would then pray for people who came forward, mostly for physical healing. Many times we saw a tremendous amount of healing in those sorts of environments—where people had been worshipping, preaching, and praying.

In the afternoon, we would take time to rest and pray before the evening meeting, which could go on late into the night. This meant that, in the afternoons, we usually stayed in our hotel rooms to take naps and rest. But Ruthie and I would sometimes go for walks during our down time. We would walk along the boardwalk near the sea in front of our hotel in the city of Fortaleza. The boardwalk is beautiful, winding along the ocean front with hotels on one side and the beach on the other. You can see the local fishermen mending their nets and repairing their boats, along with various vendors who are after the tourist dollars. It is a pretty safe area to walk in, as police officers patrol the area.

My Duck Will Die

One afternoon, Ruthie and I took off down the boardwalk for our afternoon break. We walked along the beach and soon saw a small, homeless, local street boy. Several boys were running about, but this particular boy (who was about twelve years old) stood out, because he was hopping on one foot, barely able to get around. When I took a closer look at him, I could see that his ankle was broken.

I could hear God say to me, "If my little duck does not get his wing healed, he will die." I told Ruthie what I had just heard. To get the boys' attention, we began buying them food from the local street vendor. As we got each of them a sandwich, we were able to get the attention of the wounded boy. He came up to us, and without a translator, we were able to communicate that we wanted to pray for him. He stood still and allowed this to happen.

As we prayed for him, we could see his foot—immobile in its bent and broken state—slowly change from that unnatural position to being normal again. When he realized what was happening, the boy immediately tested his ankle. He then began to walk forward carefully and then took a few more steps. Then he placed his full weight on his foot and sort of ran off with his friends, being silly, while sharing a smoke with his buddy. As he moved away, crossing the street, we saw him look back and smile.

If that was all there was to the story, it would have been an amazing testimony of God's love. But there is more! We had finished with our walk and were feeling pretty good about what had happened. We began walking back to the hotel, talking about this wonderful miracle. As we walked, we

KIDS ARE THE KEY

noticed several homeless people were waving and shouting for us to come to them. Here was this strange scene of six homeless people, arranged along the boardwalk on the benches, with one in a wheelchair. They had organized themselves into a queue, and we realized they had probably seen what had happened with the little boy. Now they wanted some healing, too.

We were awestruck that this could even happen, and we knew these people genuinely wanted a touch from God. We could not believe our eyes! We approached the group and, again with no translator, began to try to communicate with them, fully expecting a language barrier. However, one of the men, who could not speak English, somehow understood everything I said. Once he realized he was the only one who could understand, he translated what I was saying for his friends. I asked him if he could speak English, and he shook his head and said he couldn't. But he definitely understood what I was saying. I had seen this happen once before, so we continued to pray for these people, asking for their names and prayer requests. I was so taken up by the ability of the man who could 'understand what I was saying that I don't really remember who, or if any, were healed. Bless God! What an incredible walk we had that day.

Healing Flows over Five Hundred Children

Five hundred kids filled the sanctuary of a private school in Cali, Colombia. As they filed past me, God said, "Ask them, 'Did you have pain in your body, or were you sick before you came into the room, and now that you're here in the sanctuary, is the pain or sickness gone?'"

I didn't pray or tell them why I was there. I merely asked the question as God directed me to, expecting the kids to respond as kids would, but their response was surprisingly mature. They raised their hands to say that something had actually happened. I invited them to come up and describe what they had experienced, and slowly they began to line up. Some were crying, saying they could not believe the pain had left their bodies.

While this was taking place on my right, I noticed a lot of kids below and to my right on the steps of the stage. I struggled to understand what I was seeing: Children of all ages were on their knees, crying. When I asked my translator what was going on, he told me the children were repenting. As these events were unfolding, the principal of the school came up to us and said they had never experienced such a phenomenon before. The children had never even seen people repent like that before.

I start a lot of my meetings that way now. I just ask that same question before I pray or preach, and I'm always surprised by how people respond. It always begins with only a few people coming up, and then there is a surge, as each realizes that he or she is not the only one who is responding. It's a tremendous thing to have God sovereignly heal, and it causes faith to grow like wildfire.

I don't want to use the word *common*, but I usually see around 20–25 percent of the people healed when they respond honestly, and I almost always have people come to me later, after the meeting, and say, "I was afraid to say that I was healed, but…."

Eleven-Year-Old Girl Walks for the First Time

One time, in 2009, I prayed for the first person of the night in front of the stage. I could see that there was a mother and probably her sister who were carrying in a girl about eleven years old. She had obvious issues, including twisted legs that didn't operate on their own.

Truthfully, the last thing I wanted to do was pray for this girl, as her condition seemed so extreme, but they came to me expectant. For some reason, they had faith that if I prayed for the girl, she would receive her miracle.

When I first went up to them, I had no translator. "God, I have nothing to give her," I said. "God, I can't do this without You. Please heal this girl," I prayed.

Suddenly, she jumped to her feet and ran. She came running back and threw herself into her mom's lap, and they cried. I had no idea what was happening. I was sure I was going to be put on the next flight home. I frantically waved down a translator, and she asked them what was going on. The translator then said to me, "They are not sad. They are crying because the girl has never walked before." I prayed three times, and she walked better each time. Praise God!

Four-Year-Old Girl Walks

In 2014, I was ministering in Cali, Columbia, with my young team from Alaska. As the night ended, one person walked up to me and handed me her hearing aids with a big smile. She was able to communicate to me that she had been totally healed.

People were coming up to me and asking me to pray for them. I had no translator at that time. A woman handed me a girl, maybe four years old. I took the child in my arms and hugged her, and I whispered a prayer in her ear. Then, having no idea what might be wrong with her, I was satisfied that God had given her a miracle. I turned around and set the girl down on the stage. At that moment, I didn't think much of it as she ran across the stage. To my surprise, many of the people in the church erupted into cheers and claps, pointing at the girl. They were so excited! That's when I found out that this was the first time the little girl had ever walked.

A Drug Boss Is Healed

My prayer is, "God take me only to those churches, and give me only those ministry opportunities, that the western church overlooks and doesn't want to go to." These are generally very poor and small. One particular night, I was bound for the poorest, most rundown church I have been to in the violent and drug-infested murder capital—Cali, Colombia.

Even the cab drivers wouldn't take me to this place. As I sat in the back seat of a cab, I watched the cab driver, his fingers wrapped around the steering wheel so tight that his knuckles turned white, consider my request to go into this neighborhood. Then he replied, "Sorry, but I will not drive there."

After finally catching a ride, we arrived. As I shared testimonies of God healing the sick, I saw a young man standing just outside the entrance of the church, watching and listening to me speak. I had no idea who this guy was, but I got a word of knowledge for him. I pointed at him and said, "You have pain in your belly, and God is going to heal you."

Turns out this man was the big guy on the block—the boss drug dealer. He had been shot in the stomach. God healed him on the spot, and he was born again. Now he, his wife, and his family attend the church, along with his two former drug captains.

That same night, I made a new friend whose back got healed. This fellow is now well on his way to knowing in his heart who Jesus is—the Messiah. And one beautiful lady could not raise her arms, but after a boy prayed for her, up went her arms. On the same occasion, several headaches were healed, two lupus symptoms were gone, three shoulders were healed, two people were saved, and pain left the room. Bless God!

YWAM—Kona, Hawaii

I was at a beachside restaurant when a waitress came up from behind me. I had the sun in my eyes, and I couldn't see her very well, but I began to realize that God was speaking to me about her. God told me she wanted to get a new tattoo and was trying to decide whether she should or not. The waitress came back, and I said to her, "Get the tattoo."

"What did you say?" She asked.

"Get the tattoo," I repeated.

"Yeah, there's this guy in Waimea that does really good tattoos, and I want this picture on my right leg, but I am trying to decide if I should get it," she said.

"How did I know about the tattoo?" I asked.

"I have no idea," she replied. "Are you some kind of psychic?"

"Yes, in a way of speaking I am," I said.

She was taking our order, and when she returned, I went on to say that if she believed what I had just told her, would she believe what I was about to say next?

"Maybe," she replied.

I began to tell her that Jesus loves her and knows her and wants a relationship with her. I was revealing the secrets of her heart, so that she would know God loves her. I think it did more for one of my disciples who was with me than anything else.

Overlooking a volleyball court near the beach one night, I saw a YWAM mission builder that I knew. I stopped to sit down and talk with this man and his wife, and I asked him about the pain in the lower left side of his back. "How do you know about that?" the man asked.

"I'm a Christian like you, but God tells me this stuff to show people His power and love," I replied.

We then talked about forgiving someone he knew, and as he forgave, he commented on how the pain was leaving his back and that he believed he was healed. As we talked, I asked, "Is your left leg a bit shorter than your right?"

He was really blown away at that point and said, "Yeah, but how do you know these things?"

I asked him to hold out both of his feet, and I showed them to the three young men I had been discipling, who were with me. Then, as quickly as I could say, *"Watch this,"* the leg grew out as my disciples and I stood there watching the miracle take place.

YWAM Kona Mission Builders Office

I attended a meeting that was held each Monday for a group known as Trade Track. These students were at YWAM Kona to go through the YWAM Discipleship Training School (DTS). During these Mondays, other trainers and I would have opportunities to teach, share testimonies, and just talk about whatever came up.

One Monday, one of the students was asking some random questions when I asked him if he had pain in his left ribs and if it was worse when he leaned forward. He said yes, that it was causing him a lot of distress. I asked him to stand up, laid a hand on him, and commanded the pain to go. It did, and we all blessed Jesus, especially the young man who had just been healed. For several days after that, he continued to talk about how he had heard stories of God healing people, but he had never believed it could happen for him. I heard later that he told a lot of people about what happened and how he was healed. Testimonies for Jesus!

Kona Home Depot

One day, as I watched the shift change take place inside a store, several employees filed out of the break room and into the aisle where I was standing and looking at tool boxes.

I noticed one lady seemed to be in pain, and I asked her if she was alright. As the others looked on, she said her ribs hurt, and she didn't know why.

"May I pray for you?" I asked.

She said I could, while simultaneously looking at her coworkers as if silently asking what this was all about. I told her to put her hand where the pain was, and I placed my hand on hers and commanded the pain to go. I prayed twice, and then she said she had to go to work. As she walked away, she thanked me. I asked if she felt better, and she said she did. Then I asked if any of the people looking on could help me with the toolbox I was looking at. The strangest thing was, they wouldn't come near me. They gave me the strangest look, and none of them seemed interested in helping this weird guy.

Tourist Trap

I went to a coffee shop in a mall in the center of Kona one night. I was out with some of our young mission builders (disciples), just strolling along, when we decided to sample some Kona coffee. As I talked with the sales girl, I began to tell her my story. I could see she was emotionally connecting with what I was saying about getting free from drugs and alcohol. I then asked her if she wanted what I had and told her that salvation is to be born again.

"Would you like to begin following Jesus and ask Him into your heart?" I asked.

"Yes, I do," she replied. "Let's do this now!"

With the young men looking on, she prayed with me and cried a lot. A few weeks later, I took her a new Bible and a devotional.

At the Mall—Downtown Kona

I saw a man walking away from me on crutches alongside a woman, either his wife or his girlfriend. I asked God to send him back to me. In seconds, the man returned with the woman. As he struggled to mount the stairs, I waited. When he reached the top, he looked at me for a moment, and I asked him if he was in pain. He said that he was and that he and his wife were on their honeymoon.

I told the man that I could make the pain stop. I got a weird look from him, and he made a move to leave. Again I said, "I can make the pain go!"

As the mission builders looked on, he stopped and asked, "How can you do that?"

The girl looked indignantly at me, as if saying, "Yeah, right!"

I extended my hand, and as the man took hold of it, I commanded the pain to go! I then asked if it was better. The man tried walking, and he said the pain was greatly reduced. I prayed again, and it got better.

The man's wife was angry and upset. "No!" she said skeptically. "That cannot work!" She was visibly upset and truly angry that something like that could even happen. All at once, she began ranting at her husband.

We walked away. Later, I walked past this couple, who had locked horns on the sidewalk in front of the mall. As I passed, the woman was telling the man that my prayer hadn't worked, while he was telling me that it did. I walked on.

Chapter 6
INDIA, SRI LANKA, PHILIPPINES

To my surprise, I found that many of the people in a church in India were those who had experienced a demonstration of God's love first hand. They were healed, and then they joined the local church expecting more of the same.

I asked several people why they were members of that particular church, and they said they had been healed of an ailment or someone they knew had received a miracle from God at that church. Yet for some reason the people there believed that the available anointing is reserved for a select few.

Church leaders would say they had seen some healing, and yes, that's where many of the disciples had come from, but they had never seen the same amount of healing as when I was with them.

I heard this several times. After leaving India, I occasionally received emails from people I had met, usually pastors, saying that the words I gave them had come to pass, or giving me testimonies of people who were healed while I was with them.

I believe we all can pull on the anointing, and we need to!

Philippines—Sogo

I took a team of Americans from Minnesota, Oregon, California, and Alaska to the Philippines. In preparation for this first official Paragon Global team trip, I researched online for accommodations, van rentals, and so forth, doing my best to ensure that all the details were taken care of so that my team would have the trip of a lifetime. I really wanted these men and women to be comfortable so they could focus on the mission at hand and not be distracted by anything that could cause them distress. One of my first administrative decisions was to carefully choose a hotel in Manila, which I chose based simply on location, availability, and of course price.

The hotel I chose was part of a very large chain with locations all over the Philippines, and it—the SoGo hotel chain—just happened to have a hotel within walking distance of the location where we would spend the first week serving a local church.

Two months later, we arrived in the Philippines with the team, enjoying a wonderful time of *as-you-go* ministry in the airport and on the plane. We got to see God do some amazing things on the trip from Anchorage to Manila, including salvations and healings. It was so much fun to watch those who had never been to Asia take in all the sights and sounds and enjoy this incredible new place.

We were finally off to the first stop, our hotel. Racing through the streets of Manila, we safely arrived at the SoGo Hotel. I once again had the opportunity to watch the team members react to this new environment. We were on the sidewalk in a heavily populated part of town, which is typical for Manila. There were people everywhere, and the commotion was almost overwhelming—with the sounds, smells, sights, and crowded sidewalks. For a bunch of Alaskans, this was borderline chaos.

While this scene was unfolding, I couldn't help but notice a sign on the hotel. It read "SOGO: So good, So clean." That was reassuring for sure, a clean hotel. Piling into the hotel, we climbed the stairs with our suitcases, each commenting that we could have travelled a little lighter, all the while thinking about cleaning up and getting some rest.

The lobby was packed with people waiting for the line to move. Like a proud papa, I observed the team excitedly talking about the adventure and their experiences. As I was doing this, I couldn't help but notice that the walls were decorated with red hearts, balloons, and little cupids, like our Valentine's Day decorations. Then I spied a dusty, life-size nude sculpture of a woman in the corner. The decorations were old, and you could see that they had been around for some time. It was clear that the lobby mantra was all about love.

I began to scan the lobby for opportunities to minister the gospel while we waited for our room keys, and I couldn't help but notice that the place was filled with couples—young men and women. What's more, they had no suitcases. The only suitcases were the ones belonging to our team members. Upon further examination, I noticed the room had no waiting area, couches, or chairs—only red, padded, semi-private cubicles.

The couples seemed to be enjoying their time in these red, padded boxes. All of them really seemed to be in love and very affectionate. Evidently, I was learning more about this country. I had no idea they were so loving.

Checking again on the team, I saw that they were still enthralled with everything that had happened so far. And they all seemed to be in pretty good shape.

Finally, we were up at the counter, talking with the clerk about the reservations. As the hotel staff got the paperwork and room keys for the team, I could see, on the wall behind the counter, the room rates written in English on a very large board. The sign listed the hotel room rates in pesos for three-hour increments. On the same sign, it listed towel rentals, personal hygiene items, and various other toiletries that the SoGo hotel offered.

Although the team had yet to notice, I finally started to get it. Frantically, I began asking the clerk about the three-hour room rates, not waiting for an answer. Verbally, I was moving into my best puffed-up, freaked-out American Christian combat mode—composure mixed with emergency tongues, all at the same time. Looking back on this now, I can understand how this may have been hard for the average Filipino clerk to understand.

I was rapidly piecing the situation together and simultaneously getting a word of knowledge that somebody in the room was getting dizzy and was about to panic. As the clerk handed me sticky, dirty keys to rooms I no longer wanted, I knew that soon the team would begin asking questions.

It began—the wave of disturbed and vocal observations from the team and the very real possibility that we might not have many accommodation options at that hour. I began negotiating with the staff, asking to see the rooms and enquiring if I could prepay so I didn't have to come to the lobby in my pajamas every three hours to keep topping up the fee. I was also sensing that the word of knowledge for an impending panic attack was becoming more intense, and I was sure that someone was about to black out at any moment.

Before me, the hotel staff seemed to be animated, appearing like a blurry, bizarre performance on the other side of the counter as they faded in and out of focus. It was apparent they had never had a group of homeless American missionaries in their house of ill repute before. The situation was a first time for us as well.

Shopping Mall in Manila

In a shopping mall in Manila, Philippines, I was riding the escalator to a lower floor when I heard a stranger behind me say to his friend, "My knee hurts so bad!"

I looked over my shoulder and could see that he was indicating that it hurt when he bent his knee. While still on the escalator, I turned quickly, put my hand on his knee and said, "Pain go in Jesus' name!" The young man looked at me in surprise!

As quickly as I started praying, I was finished, and at about the same time, we had arrived at the lower floor. As we got off the escalator, the young man said, "Hey, the pain is gone!" This gave me the perfect opportunity to tell him about my Jesus—the Jesus who made a way for me to know my Father God.

I asked if I could pray for him again, and he said *yes*. As I prayed, I said these words: "Thank You, God, for sending Your son, Jesus, to take sin from the world so that those who believe that Jesus is Your son and that He died for us on the cross may have everlasting life with You. Thank You for helping us know that by turning away from sin and asking for forgiveness, living a life of faith and works, we can have salvation. Thank You, God, for demonstrating Your love for this young man by healing his knee."

God healed the boy, and I preached the gospel. Jesus is grace, and this is what it looks like for believers to have grace living inside of them. Grace is Jesus, who by the Holy Spirit enables us to demonstrate His love.

> *For it is by grace you have been saved, through faith— and this is not from yourselves, it is the gift of God— not by works, so that no one can boast. For we are God's handiwork, created in Christ Jesus to do good works, which God prepared in advance for us to do* (Ephesians 2:8–10).

This is our sufficiency: *"My grace is sufficient for you..."* (2 Cor. 12:9) *"God is able to make all grace about to you, so that having all sufficiency in all things at all times, you may abound in every good work"* (2 Cor. 9:8 ESV).

At an open air meeting in the Philippines, I saw a man standing by his office window hundreds of feet away. I pointed at him and said, "You have pain in your back!"

He nodded and said, "Yes I do!"

Then I commanded the pain to go. He walked to the stage and gave his life to Jesus on the spot.

Park and Pray

We also spent time praying for people where they park their motorcycles. What an unexpected experience for people to meet God during the course of their day. Many Philippine people were healed, set free, and delivered!

Sri Lanka

I was invited to hold a Signs, Miracles, and Wonders meeting in Sri Lanka, just outside of the capital city, Colombo. I loved the scene—a room with a colorful, heavily padded carpet where the people would sit. People found their way into the room and sat about—smiling, talking, and looking at me and wondering how the night would unfold. I could tell they were expectant about the meeting.

As I began speaking, I noticed a rough looking man entering the room, obviously from some alley of the lowest caste. As he came forward, he awkwardly, hesitantly and carefully stepped around the people.

I could see that he didn't belong to this family of believers, and it was almost as if he was forcing himself into a place on the floor directly in front of me. He was noticeably deformed, a grotesque looking man. His right shoulder seemed as if it had grown into the center of his chest, and he was almost bent in two, with his head and neck pulling down to his shoulder. He was deformed, dirty, and maybe in need of deliverance.

It was challenging, to say the least, to have a man so badly in need of a full-on miracle on every level. The meeting continued, God performed many miracles, and faith was rising. Meanwhile, I could not get this man out of my head. Everything about him was distracting. While closing the meeting and thanking God for the evening, I asked the congregation to pray for the needs of others.

My driver and the pastor quickly came to this man and prayed, laying hands on him. That evening's topic was mostly about forgiveness, and as this man forgave, his body began to unfold, and his arm came away from his chest. He was a revised man, smiling, and as he moved closer, I could see his full face while he stood proudly, both shoulders back, as if at attention.

After interviewing him, I found out that he did indeed live among the lowest caste and that he had been deformed like that for years. I could only imagine what this would say to the people he knew—his family and friends. Jesus!

Chapter 7
RIGHT HERE IN THE USA

Mysteries, Miracles, and Mr. X

At a small prayer gathering, I shared the testimony of how a friend of a man who was present there was radically and miraculously healed when I prayed over him. The man had regained mobility in his neck, where previously he had restricted movement due to fused vertebrae and metal plates. I told the gathering of how this man, who was now completely healed, had shared a video testimony with me in which he demonstrated the range of movement that had been restored to his neck and talked of how he had been delivered from the pain he had previously suffered.

As I told the story, Tom—the man who had witnessed the miracle—confirmed the validity of my words as he praised God. I could see faith being fanned into flame in my listeners as Tom and I testified about the miracle. I continued to pray for people in the gathering to experience God's incredible power and salvation.

That's when the man sitting next to Tom, a man I didn't know, asked if I would pray for him. He said he had the same condition as the person I was talking about; he also had metal plates and screws in his neck. I did as the man requested and prayed for him.

"Your hands are warm, and I can feel something taking place in my neck," he said.

I hear this comment frequently, but it doesn't always indicate immediate, radical healing. However, when I stopped praying, the man said he was feeling better than before, and the mobility in his neck had improved. He seemed excited and encouraged by the experience.

The meeting continued, and I kept praying over people. Others were also healed, and we all went home praising God. The next day, Tom's friend sent me a video testimony of how he had been healed. How incredible that he had heard me share a testimony of a miracle that took place two years before, asked me to pray for him for the same condition, and received healing as well. I was amazed by the goodness of God and was excited that I now had two videos from men who had been blessed by the same miracle.

This story is significant, and you will understand just how significant it is when you see it in the light of what I experienced two years prior to that prayer gathering where the second man was healed.

My friend, Tom, had taken me to an native village in Alaska and introduced me to some people there. He was hoping I would pray for them as God led me to and that God would reveal Himself in ways these good people had never believed was possible. They had never had personal experiences of God's power and love.

I was invited to a native funeral, called a Potlatch, and while I there, I sat for a while by myself, aware that I was one of the very few white men present. At the same time, I also realized that I was probably more native than some others in the room, but was definitely perceived as white. At that moment I felt very white, too, because of the fistful of dried mystery meat that I had just been given from a cardboard box that was being passed around. I didn't know what to do with it.

As I continued to sit by myself, a large native man spotted me. He stared at me for a while and then came over to where I was seated. I wasn't quite sure what was about to take place and was actually a bit alarmed because of the sheer size of the man. In a moment of human weakness, I considered the possibility that he might be the town bully who was coming to enquire as to why I hadn't eaten the meat that I still had in my hand.

The man sat down next to me, introduced himself, and asked my name. He smiled as he talked and seemed to be a really nice person who was genuinely happy I was there and didn't want me to sit by myself, looking like I was afraid I might be the next to go into the mystery meat box.

I looked around the room and noticed that the other men were passing around a rifle, while others were eating a kind of potato salad and gnawing on the dried meat. I turned to the large man and asked, a little nervously, if he had carpal tunnel in his wrist. After the usual response—"How did you know that?"—I gave him a general explanation and seized the opportunity to pray for him.

The man was healed on the spot and was a bit shocked by what had just occurred. He immediately went off to find Tom and told him what had taken place. That was when I found out that I wasn't invited to pray over people at the

Potlatch, as they weren't open to such things. I had been brought to meet with a select group of people that Tom knew, and obviously I hadn't received this information in the briefing before. Thankfully, all was well, and the big man who sought me out at the gathering was healed.

After this event, Tom and I went to the place where we were to stay the night. As we arrived, we were greeted by a man whose name I cannot reveal, and so I will call him Mr. X. Tom and I sat up talking to Mr. X until about 3 am. We talked about many different things, including how God "broke" Mr. X's neck.

Yes, those were Mr. X's exact words. He told me that God was teaching him about perseverance. I didn't say a word or give him a disapproving look. I didn't move a muscle. I just sat and listened. This was completely out of character for me, but God had a plan, and when He told me to make my move, I leapt at the opportunity.

During a pause in the conversation, I got to my feet and asked where the bathroom was. I began to walk past Mr. X, but instead of moving past him, I spun around, put my hand on Mr. X's neck, and commanded the metal in his neck, "Go! And pain, go!" I then began to speak about things I had no prior knowledge of—about Mr. X being unable to sleep, how he would be tossing and turning all night because of the pain and discomfort. I prayed over these things, and Mr. X just sat there, surprised, and politely allowed me to go on with what I was doing. Tom walked into the room and witnessed this event and praised God. Thereafter, Mr. X thanked me and retired to bed.

The next morning, I walked into the kitchen to see Mr. X and Tom laughing over a cup of coffee. As I entered, Mr. X joyfully told me that he had been healed the previous night and had slept like a baby. He immediately demonstrated for me his new range of movement and told me he wanted the world to know that God still moves and heals today. That day we got a video testimony of Tom interviewing Mr. X talking about God's amazing power and love.

Thereafter, Tom and I were excited to go and visit another friend and deliver a gang banger from a demon before we returned home to Wasilla. Praise God for that amazing time in the village. Our faith was just soaring after witnessing God heal the neck of Mr. X. The man was so excited and alive, and spoke about how good it was to have his mobility back. For him, this encounter with God was unimaginable one before. As we drank coffee with him that morning, he would go on to talk with excitement about the future.

At Lowes

While at Lowes one day, I helped a man load building materials onto his cart. As he shook my hand, I got a word of knowledge that he suffered from back pain. I asked him if he had pain in his back, as I placed my hand on the exact spot, and he said, "Yes, for years."

"I have an app for that," I said, while reaching out to take his hand.

The moment he took my hand, I began to pray, "God of heaven and earth," I said, and then paused to give him an opportunity to stop me or to let me continue. He gave me an approving look, as if to say, "Let's do this!"

I prayed quickly and simply. Then, letting go of his hand, I asked how he felt. He said he was surprised to say that he felt a lot better. I then asked about the shoulder pain and prayed for that, too. He was grateful that his back and shoulder pain had disappeared. I had an opportunity to talk with him a bit in the checkout line and left hoping that he felt loved.

All of this took place in front of one of my disciples who had been praying to operate in the gifts and was disappointed to somehow not get what he had asked for. This was very timely, as he saw firsthand that he had to trust God and step into the opportunities He sets before him. I told him that if he wanted to see a lot of healing, he would have to pray for a lot of people. I am glad to report that now this young man walks mightily in the word and power of Jesus.

Other Cool Healings

I prayed for a paraplegic in Florida. He went out in the spirit, and his nurse thought he was sick or dying. She tried to revive him while I quietly exited the room.

In Los Angeles, California, I got a word of knowledge for my Uber driver about the pain he was experiencing when he worked out and that he guarded himself against the pain. I prayed for him, and he was healed while driving.

Many times, at meetings, I have pulled ladies to their feet—kind of like a spin dance—and they got healed. God is fun!

On one occasion, at a crusade, a team member who was on the platform interrupted me during the meeting. He had had a vision that if I waved my hand, 250 people would be healed. So I did it, and they were!

At the Street Ministry in Anchorage, Alaska, in just one night, one person was delivered of a pain in the leg, while a man felt like he was lifted up and had hope restored, and another person was delivered from muscle pain in the left foot. I love praying for the people there and seeing them touched by the finger of God. People kept thanking us for giving them clothes and food and for taking the time to love them.

Chapter 8
BAGGAGE CLAIMS AND AIRPLANES

Russia

The speed with which I took my seat had caused me to forget to say my standard airplane prayer, in which I ask for a divine appointment during the flight. As I sat back in my seat, my thoughts went back to the time I had just spent in Petropavlovsk, Russia, where I had been involved in meetings with church leaders. One meeting had been scheduled solely to deliver money that our church was contributing to help with the new church heating system. I couldn't believe I had spent two thousand dollars of my money to do this.

As the plane began to taxi, I couldn't help but notice about two inches of fresh snow on the wings, and I guessed that de-icing was not as high of a priority here as it is in the United States. Perhaps some airline or government official had decided it was just not worth the additional costs, I mused. I found myself praying during the entire take off, hoping that when we arrived in Moscow ten hours later there would be the same applause from the passengers as there had been when we landed in Petropavlovsk.

My time in Russia had been less than interesting, as I had spent much of it talking about the church's new heating system. The one bright spot was getting the opportunity to pray with people at the Sunday church service and seeing God heal a few. That, for me, made the trip seem worthwhile, along with the recurrence of a dream about that church, which God had originally given me a year earlier when I had been in Brazil.

I had been walking about the construction site one day, and I asked God, "What am I doing here?" As soon as I spoke the words, the dream—or vision—appeared like it had before, and I realized this was the place I had dreamt of before—the building in an unfinished state.

I could remember from the dream, in which I stood on the unfinished stage, that this was the same vantage point from which the dream unfolded. In the dream, the auditorium was large and could possibly seat five to six hundred people, maybe more. The floors sloped upward and were of bare concrete, while in the vision the floor was the same, but one day the seats would be red, and there would be long red drapes hanging all around the sanctuary.

The vision reminded me that I would stand on that stage as people were healed, especially those in the front rows, to my right, who were in the section for the hearing impaired.

Sitting in my seat in the airplane, as I listened to a Danny Silk podcast, I couldn't help but notice that directly across the aisle from me was a couple with their baby boy. The baby was crying, and he continued crying as the plane took off. The child's incessant crying had intensified, and the parents tried everything to calm the infant down—giving him a bottle, burping him, offering him food, trying a diaper change, walking him and then sitting with him—but their efforts were in vain. The crying persisted.

I tried unsuccessfully to drown out the sound of the infant's non-stop bawling by turning up the volume on my iPod, but the noise was becoming more annoying and unbearable. I said to God, "Somebody has got to do something about this!"

And that's when I heard God say, "That somebody is you."

"Jesus," I silently exclaimed, "I don't speak Russian. What should I do?"

Without a clue as to what I should do, I took my head phones off, unbuckled my seatbelt, and was soon standing in front of the father of the crying infant. I still had no idea what I was going to do.

I quickly discovered that the parents of the crying child knew even less English than I knew Russian, so I jumped into American charades combined with a mixture of body language gestures and hand puppet maneuvers, while blurting out unrecognizable Russian phrases. All this to try to convey that I was asking permission to pray for the little boy, who was screaming in agony. They were obviously unable to interpret what I was trying to communicate through my bizarre and possibly frightening demonstration. I was getting nowhere.

I didn't know what else to do. I may have panicked, as the next thing I knew, I was yanking the boy from his father's arms. I was surprised that he so easily allowed me to take the boy. He must have been awed by my ability to communicate at such a high level. Now I had the baby in my arms while his mother was trying, while still buckled, to leap to her feet and grab her son. Meanwhile, the father of the child was holding his wife back, and I was wondering what exactly I was doing. And what I was going to do next.

The parents of the crying boy were looking at me in astonishment, desperate for their child to feel better and stop crying. I just stood there holding him, eyes locked with his parents. And the child stopped screaming. "Thank You, Jesus," I said. I held him for a while longer as he settled down, and I prayed, using Jesus' name a lot and whatever Russian words I knew to bless God, hoping that would give them a clue as to how the miracle had taken place.

By that time, the baby's mother was crying and still trying to get at me to take her child. As soon as the infant stopped crying, I handed him back to his father.

The couple had their child back and were looking at me in amazement. To this day, I'm certain they had no idea what I kept repeating in my limited Russian, but I trust the Holy Spirit will make my meaning clear to them. For the rest of the flight, the family shied away from any further contact with me.

It was apparent that they couldn't quite explain what had happened with their child, and they didn't want to know more about what had taken place. No attempts were made to have the flight crew translate. They seemed eager to put that particular incident behind them. It was like we had just robbed a bank together, and we would, from that point on, pretend like it had never even happened. When we landed in Moscow, the passengers did applaud.

The following year, I returned to Russia to help install the in-floor heating system in the main sanctuary. Arriving at the church, I was fixated on the section of the sanctuary reserved for the hearing impaired.

We began to lay the tubing, and I recall looking back and seeing how unusually I had performed the task at hand. It was very clear that when I laid the tubing in that area, I was not thinking about in-floor heat. It took us several days to get all the tubing installed, and I had a great time trying to learn Russian, as my counterpart tried to learn English. I also kept going back to the section for the hearing impaired, just to see the tubing layout, since we had only a few more days left in Russia.

I was invited to speak at the youth group church service. In the room, there were probably just thirty people. We were welcomed, someone preached a little, and then I was given an opportunity to speak.

I had absolutely no idea what I was supposed to do that night. I was unprepared, and without any plan in mind. So I stood up, introduced myself, and began to prophesy over the people counter clockwise around the room. Immediately, I recognized the accuracy of the prophetic words I was speaking. I knew the dreams in people's hearts, their secrets, and their occupations. This was probably the first time that I had prophesied so accurately over so many people.

By the end of the night, we were all amazed by God's power. I wanted to break this incredible news to my pastor before anyone from the Russian church could contact him about what had just happened. And I also wanted to ensure that I remained grounded and humble.

The next morning, the word was out that I was a prophet, and everyone treated me in a radically different manner from the way they had the day before. The pastor acted like he was standing before a throne, and it was embarrassing. I was treated differently by the workers as well, once they discovered they were in the presence of a prophet.

I went through the next few days trying not to let this go to my head. On the morning of my departure, I was taken to the church office, where I was greeted by all of the church staff and the elders with the most incredible breakfast I've ever seen in my life. It was immaculate. We were dining on foods that very few Russians had probably ever seen. I remember watching the church staff enjoy this meal to honor me and the gift on my life, and I was very grateful and tried to thank them several times.

Baggage Claim Healing

Just after arriving in Sao Polo, Brazil, as I waited near the baggage claim for my suitcase to arrive, I devoted my time to watching other people and their bags go by. This was an interesting place to observe how people reacted to their surroundings, as they jockeyed for position (so they could stand as close as possible to the device that would soon deliver their luggage) and eventually dragged their overstuffed bags off the carousel.

My bag was nowhere in sight, but I could tell that the lady next to me had seen hers and was about to make her move to retrieve this wheeled wonder—a floral, over-stuffed, bulging suitcase that obviously was too heavy for her. I considered offering to help, but before I could even begin rescue efforts, she had grabbed the bag, rolled it off the carousel, and dropped it onto her foot.

She stood there in silent agony, a lot of pain on her face, possibly cursing in some foreign language. Then, with a foul look, she turned and voiced her displeasure in another language to the man behind her, who had also watched the entire event unfold.

I was a little surprised by what took place next. This lady looked directly at me, waiting expectantly, as if I had some grand solution to her pain. She continued to look at me as if I was withholding the pain relief that she was fully expecting, almost as if she knew me somehow as the guy with the answer. I looked at both of them and asked myself if I knew these people. Perhaps they had been to one of my healing services? Did they know me as someone who could pray and release God's healing to her?

Unable to communicate with her verbally, I rapidly thought about what I should do. With some kind of bizarre international sign language, I managed to convince her to put her foot up on the edge of the baggage carousel in front of us. Once her foot was in position, so I would not have to kneel on the floor, I placed my hand on her foot and commanded healing. The entire time, she and her husband looked at me as if this was exactly what needed to happen.

Soon she was smiling! Then she glanced at her husband, and off they went. They walked away as if what had just happened was normal, as if that is just what people do when they get hurt—ask someone to pray and get healed by God.

Saved at Thirty Thousand Feet

We were on our way to Brazil, and just minutes before boarding our flight, I experienced what I now know was an open vision. It was like watching a short video in which I was in the cockpit of a commercial jet airliner praying with the co-pilot.

The vision filled me with a sense of expectancy as I boarded the aircraft, and I could hardly wait to enter and look into the cockpit. I followed my wife as we stepped into the airplane, but as she moved right, down the aisle to find her seat, I turned left and looked inside the cockpit. Even as I did, the co-pilot saw me and waved me in. I eagerly responded to his invitation without even saying a word to my wife.

I introduced myself to the co-pilot and told him why I was in Brazil. Then, recalling the vision, I prayed for him and the flight. I turned to leave, as I would need to take my seat, and came face to face with the captain. I quickly, and very nervously, explained what I was doing in the cockpit and mentioned that I had just prayed for the co-pilot and the flight. The pilot told me that the co-pilot would show me how to use the jump seat and that I would be flying up front with them to the next city.

Having delivered this surprising statement, the captain turned, clip board in hand, and left the cockpit. I looked at the co-pilot, and he looked back at me in surprise. "This is against international law, and every member of this crew could be fired if you're caught flying in the jump seat. But if the captain wants you to fly with us, then I guess you are," he said.

I thought to myself, I don't care if everyone gets fired. I'm not passing up this opportunity to fly with the captain. You could have threatened to shoot a few of the crew and you still would not have been able to drag me out of the cockpit.

A short while later, when we were airborne, it struck me that neither my wife nor the leadership of our team had the slightest idea where I was. I asked the captain if he could perhaps send someone to inform my wife of my whereabouts. Moments later, the steward found my wife and said to her, "Your husband is a very important man, and he will be flying with the captain today."

A short while into our flight, the captain slid his seat back and said to me, "I have met a lot of Christians in my life, but none like you. I asked you to fly with me so I can learn what makes you tick."

"You're going to be grilled," I heard God say clearly. "If you don't know the answer, just say, 'I don't know.'"

The captain asked me a series of questions, and I shared my testimony. He asked me about hearing from God, what a personal relationship with Him was like, and many other questions. Many of my answers were, "I don't know." The captain and co-pilot were astounded by the relationship I had with Jesus and amazed that they could be in a real relationship with Him as well.

By this time, I was out of my seat and kneeling on the floor in front of the control panel between the two pilots. Offering an upturned hand to each of them, I asked the question, "Do you want what I have?" Without hesitation, both men placed their hands in mine and began to repeat a prayer asking for forgiveness for sin and receiving salvation.

The plane landed, and the captain and I greeted the passengers as they left the plane. I said to our team, "Thank you for flying TAM Airlines today! Bye! Enjoy your day!"

I was sure my face would split from smiling as our team walked past me, standing there with the captain, overwhelmed by joy that he and his co-pilot had just accepted Jesus as their Lord and Savior.

Other Airplane Stories

When I took my seat on a flight for Cali, Colombia, I noticed a small, elderly Spanish lady sitting in the middle seat. She was really old, and a younger woman was sitting next to her in the window seat. I sat down, and the plane departed. As we flew, I began to get a word of knowledge. I asked God who this was for, and He said it was for the elderly lady. I asked her if she spoke English, and she indicated that she didn't. I asked the younger lady in the next seat, and she said she did, so I asked if she would translate for me, and she agreed.

Through my translator, I asked the elderly lady if she had pain in her back. She said she did, and my interpreter explained what she was saying to me about the pain. I asked her if I could ask Jesus to take the pain away, and she indicated that it would be OK. Before we prayed, I asked my interpreter if she believed, and she shook her head and said, "No." This actually made me really happy, because in a few minutes these two people were going to be believers. We prayed, and the elderly lady said she was totally healed. Praise God! The younger lady next to her on the airplane, while an unbeliever, acted as my interpreter—and the woman was healed!

On another flight from Anchorage to Seattle, two people seated next to me had boarded the plane very drunk and loud. I told them, in the nicest way possible, that if they kept it up they could be removed from the flight. When they continued to be obnoxious and loud, I rebuked the spirit of alcohol in Jesus' name, and they both fell silent. I prophesied about them and their children, describing for one man the gender and age of his child. One of them cried when I prophesied what an amazing father he was going to be.

They both began asking me what I had just done. And another passenger who sat in the row in front of us began asking who I was. I introduced myself, but I clarified that it was Jesus who had touched them. Then, after a few minutes, they were again drunk and loud. It was not as bad as before, but they were still noticeably drunk. When we landed, I spent maybe two hours with one of the passengers, talking to him about Jesus. It turned out he had walked away from God and was now rethinking that decision.

On another flight, I sat next to a woman who told me she was miserable. I talked with her, and she said she wanted the real thing. So I played her a Kim Walker album on my iPhone. This lady cried for the entire flight.

A stewardess walked by me several times on a flight, and God told me He wanted to heal her wrist. I mustered the confidence to go and tell her that God wanted to heal her wrist, and she said, "Yes, please, go ahead!" The other stewardess immediately said, "I'm next!" because she was also in pain.

On another flight, I told the stewardess that God had told me she was hoping to start a business in cosmetics. It was like she could not believe her ears. I told her that God reveals the secrets of people's hearts to me so that they will believe in Him. She said she was also a Christian and that she had never imagined that someone would confirm what she was dreaming of doing. At the end of the flight, she came back to me and said that because of what I had told her she had decided to go for it and start the business she had been dreaming of.

Chapter 9
ON THE JOB

While on the job, I often see miracles. Once, a carpenter I had never met before, who was a former gang member, happened to walk by me on the steps. As we passed each other, I touched his back with my finger and told him exactly where he had a pain. He got healed and gave his life to Jesus.

Crawl Space

While installing a water heater in the crawlspace of a new customer, I seized the opportunity to talk with the man, and like always, the conversation became all about Jesus.

As we talked, I learned that this man attended a local Baptist church. Soon he was telling me that he wanted the baptism of the Holy Spirit, too. I had known this man for about two hours, and I had just finished installing his new water heater. We were sitting in the dirt under his house. The fruit of all my story telling was that he was asking about the Holy Spirit. In short, we talked through the following verses:

> *While Apollos was at Corinth, Paul took the road through the interior and arrived at Ephesus. There he found some disciples and asked them, "Did you receive the Holy Spirit when you believed?" They answered, "No, we have not even heard that there is a Holy Spirit." So Paul asked, "Then what baptism did you receive?" "John's baptism," they replied. Paul said, "John's baptism was a baptism of repentance." He told the people to believe in the one coming after him, that is, in Jesus." On hearing this, they were baptized in the name of the Lord Jesus. When Paul placed his hands on them, the Holy Spirit came on them, and they spoke in tongues and prophesied* (Acts 19:1–6).

After sharing these verses with him, I laid a hand on the man's shoulder and invited the Holy Spirit.

Divine Appointment

Backing slowly out of the driveway in my plumbing truck, I couldn't take my eyes off my customer, who was playing in the front yard with his grandkids. I had just completed a boiler repair, and as I drove away, I was asking God out loud, "Why haven't I had any real access to this man or his family?" I had barely talked with him and had had no opportunity to enter into any kind of conversation, yet God had told me about a divine appointment with this man.

Several months later, I got a call from this man's wife. She told me their hot water heater was leaking, and she wanted to schedule an appointment to have it repaired. While she was speaking, I heard God say, "This is the one," and I was thinking, *Here it is! The long-promised divine appointment!* I could hardly wait to go to their home.

As soon as I entered my customer's house, I saw this man sitting in his living room recliner with his feet elevated. He was wearing a big, black, nylon removeable cast on his left foot. On the inside, I was shouting, *Hallelujah! Jesus, You love me so much!*

My heart racing, I set my tools down and asked the man what had happened to him. He began to tell me about an auto accident. Someone had decided to commit suicide in their car; that person had swerved, crossed the center line, and hit his car head on. He said he had had no chance to respond, and he woke up in the hospital.

A lot was happening while he told his story. My mind was racing, and I was asking God what He wanted me to do about this situation. The first thought I had was, "Talk about forgiveness." So I took time to explain how we can forgive people and that we need to. In the midst of the conversation, he told me that he was a Christian and mentioned the church he attended.

I finally felt like the man had genuinely forgiven the person who had caused his accident as I helped him ask the Holy Spirit to assist him through the process of forgiveness. I continued to pray and to command healing, still very much filled with faith that this was a divine appointment, just as God had told me so many months earlier.

I prayed boldly and with much faith, saying, "God is going to heal you!"

The man said, "Yeah, but lots of people are praying for me, and I'm sure I will be better after the surgery."

I then asked him about the surgery. He told me that the doctor had said there was a 13 percent chance that he would die during the procedure. I cancelled the words as fast as they came out of the man's mouth, and I kept praying, even as he said that many people were praying for him.

Now, there was always the possibility I might lose the project I hadn't even begun yet. These things can and do happen. But I was also aware that God is my source and supply. He is my priority, and I need to trust Him with everything. So I interrupted the man as he talked, and I asked him how his foot felt. I never thought we would get to this part. He replied, "Well, it doesn't hurt right now."

I then asked him if he would allow me to take his cast off so he could test his foot. His wife had by then run out of the room, intentionally displaying her disapproval around the time that I began to command healing, and I hadn't seen her since. The man agreed, so I got working on getting the cast off, and the man gingerly got out of his chair and walked around his living room without any pain. When he sat down again, I began to prophesy over him that he would be able to sleep comfortably once more, that the pain in his chest would be gone, and that he would be able to sleep on his back again.

After I replaced the water heater, immersed in my prayer language the entire time, the man paid the bill and then asked me to return the next day and replace a faucet. I did as he asked the following day, and the man then told me that he couldn't fathom how I had known about his chest problems and the fact that he couldn't sleep on his back. He went on to tell me that he had slept the entire night without any chest pain. He also revealed that his attention had been so focused on the pain in his chest and left foot that he hadn't realized he also had a pain in his right foot. "Could you pray for that, too?" he asked. I did, and the pain was instantly gone. However, this man still couldn't connect the dots and see that my laying hands on him had led to his healing.

Conversations with the man's wife were also improving a little, but praying for her wasn't necessary. She called me one afternoon and said that she and her husband had just left the doctor's office and that the doctor could find no evidence that her husband had ever had an accident or suffered injuries. The doctor had used the word miracle no less than three times. And now, instead of having a surgery that involved a 13 percent chance of her husband dying, they were going to celebrate life by buying airplane tickets and going on vacation.

I Have an App for That

I had just repaired another water heater, and as I picked up my tools, my customer—a construction mechanic—suddenly began to tell me about a frost bite that he suffered a year ago, which had left his finger numb and tingly.

I said, "I have an app for that!"

My customer began to laugh, and as he laughed, I quickly reached out, grabbed his finger, and said, "Be healed in Jesus' name!"

Even as I made the move, I was afraid I might have made a mistake. The guy was bigger than me, and what's more, I hadn't yet been paid! My life literally flashed before my eyes as I held on to this big guy's finger.

As I stood looking up at this very large man, I noticed that he appeared to be holding his breath as he observed my feeble attempt to look fearless and confident. He then released what I thought was his last breath before he pounded me into the carpet. This gave me the opportunity to let go of his finger, and as I let go, he said, "My finger is no longer numb! It hasn't felt like this for a whole year!"

My customer then revealed to me that he was a Christian, but he had never experienced anything like that before. I took the opportunity to tell him some of my story and how I had made the decision to give my life to Jesus and be grateful. I told him that listening to God's voice and doing what He says is one of the ways I demonstrate my belief that God is who He says He is. In this way, I demonstrate His power and salvation as in Matthew 10:7–8.

I Have an App for That #2

While I was at a job, my customer came into the room where I was working and began to complain to me about several surgeries and pain in his back. I silently thanked God. Quickly getting to my feet, I approached him, taking my phone out of my pocket, and I said, "I have an app for that!" I opened my phone and pushed it toward his face so that his attention was on the device. I watched as he squinted at it, trying to make out what I was talking about.

As he took the phone from me, I put my hand on his back and commanded the pain to go. I then asked him how his back felt and if the pain was gone. He bent over a few times to test it out and told me that the pain, which had troubled him for years, was now gone.

When the initial surprise wore off, he asked me, "What's with this app you told me about?"

"Umm… well, you see, I just needed to distract you long enough to be able to lay my hands on you for your back to be healed. You see, I didn't want your unbelief to mess with your healing, so I distracted you with the phone. And I didn't ask to pray for you, because I didn't want to invite your unbelief."

Knee Healed

One day, after I had completed the installation of a water heater for my seventy-two-year-old customer, Jane, I sat with her at her kitchen table while I wrote out her invoice. As she was about to make out a check for the work, I said out loud,

"Come, Holy Spirit!" She asked me what I had just said, and when I told her, she gave me a strange look.

Then I said, "God is about to heal your knee. The anointing for healing is here." She gave me another weird look, because she hadn't told me anything about her knee. I repeated the words, "Come, Holy Spirit," and then I asked her if it was OK for me to place my hand on her knee. She said it was, and I moved my finger to the exact spot on her knee where the pain was. I asked her, "Do you feel that?" She said she did. God was rearranging the damaged tissue under my hand. She welled up and almost cried when she tried her knee and realized it was healed. Bless Jesus!

Hungry People

One day I was talking with a customer, a young man. As I wrote out his invoice for the plumbing work I had done for him, I told him about the amazing plan God has for his life. As I spoke, I could see he was longing for a word about his destiny. The short and simple truth was that he felt loved. It was possible that no one had ever painted a picture like that for him, and he was probably quite surprised that I was not judgmental or critical of the choices he had made up to that point. We shook hands as I left the job site.

What really struck me was that he didn't want to let go of my hand. He was grateful that I had talked to him and told him how God sees him, and he easily received the gospel of Jesus as I told him about the price that was paid, why it was paid, and who it was paid for.

People are hungry for a non-religious Jesus who loves and is not critical, and they will also receive the gospel full on. There is no other name by which you must be saved other than *Jesus!*

Faith Building

Meeting a new customer, who wanted to have a new water heater installed, I found that he was suffering and in pain, so I showed him some of the video testimonies I had collected from people who had received the healing of Jesus. These testimonies were very much a faith builder. We prayed, and though there were no outward signs or overwhelming sensations of the Holy Spirit, he believed that God wanted to heal him. Many times I feel like the real miracle is that I overcame fear that wasn't mine.

Salvation Leads to a Contract

A construction contractor contacted our plumbing and heating company to hire us to carry out a project simply because the owner had heard of a physical healing that took place on a job site from my word of knowledge and prayer. This led directly to a young man's salvation!

Never Holding Back

Not long ago, I installed a water heater for a same-sex couple. I was so pleased with myself that I never had a judgmental thought in my head and treated these folks with respect. After I made the installation and they had paid the bill, I had an opportunity to pray for the couple. I just asked if I could. One of them had severe pain. After I prayed, they thanked me and said that it was very bold of me to pray for them.

Pray the gospel. As you pray, thank God for His Son, thank God for the life that Jesus lived, demonstrating what it could be like to have a close relationship with God. Thank God that He gave His only Son to die for forgiveness of our sins, and pray up one side of the cross and down the other until the miracle and power of resurrection come out of your mouth, revealing the way, the truth, the life—Jesus Christ! As it says in the Bible, *"Salvation is found in no one else, for there is no other name under heaven given to mankind by which we must be saved"* (Acts 4:12).

All of us were in tears that day, and the two ladies hugged me and thanked me for telling them about Jesus. I suppose seeds were planted. More so, I think it was for me. God broke my judgmental heart. He wants me to see people the way He does. God loves and desires that all will know Him, that none should perish. As it says in 2 Peter 3:9, *"The Lord is not slow in keeping his promise, as some understand slowness. Instead he is patient with you, not wanting anyone to perish, but everyone to come to repentance."*

Just Another Day in My Life

Customer #1: A home owner was grieving the loss of a loved one. After I gave her a word of knowledge about a headache on the left side that she had had every day since the loss, she agreed, as I prayed with her, to give the pain of the loss to Jesus. And the migraine completely disappeared!

Customer #2: I got a word of knowledge for a tenant and told her what she had been seeking God about in secret. She began to cry immediately. I told her that God loves her and to keep seeking Him.

Customer #3: A conversation turned to a testimony of what God had done in my life.

Customer #4: I prayed for physical healing for another customer, and that person was very appreciative. I also asked someone to forgive me.

Set Up

One time, I took on a customer that a fellow plumbing company didn't have time for. They recommended me, and I started this home project that went on for over three years. I was regularly coming to this home to further my part of the project, but I found that, because the owners were professionals, the family was never at home. I received most of my directions for the project in writing or via an occasional phone call, with very little personal contact. This scenario caused me to constantly ask God when I would have an opportunity to help this family encounter Him.

A few times on this project, some of the employees had encounters. One particular carpenter had a brace on his wrist, and God healed him, to his surprise, which was really amazing. But even as I prayed for the man, I just kept wondering when I would get a chance to meet with the customers that I had barely seen over the three years. When the project was complete, I continued to service my customer's heating system once a year.

One day, the homeowner called asking me to come and carry out the annual servicing of the boiler. She told me that her mother was visiting and would open the door for me. This was unusual, as I had the alarm code and normally just let myself in, but I didn't express my surprise, and we set up an appointment day and time.

The next day when I arrived for the scheduled service call, an elderly lady opened the front door and looked straight at me. She was very ill and began gasping for breath, stumbling backwards awkwardly, almost fainting and falling back into a chair. I caught her just in time and helped her into the chair.

The lady, really unwell and gasping for breath, was trying to tell me about her condition. She said it was called Pleurisy and that it made breathing extremely painful for her. I began to pray for her without asking permission. And I laid hands on this lady—my customer's mother—as I prayed. Soon she started to look better and said she was all right. I told her a little about what Jesus had done in my life, and she told me a little about her church. Then I went off and worked on the boiler.

The next Sunday at church, in the foyer, I just happened to see my customer and her mother walking toward me. I was very surprised to see the two of them at my church, and I asked my customer's mother how she was doing, even as I expressed my surprise at seeing them there. The answer they gave me came as a great surprise.

My customer, the elderly lady's daughter, told me that I had been set up. She said she had heard about me, and the main reason she called me wasn't to have me service her boiler. She said she had called because she just knew that when I was at her home I would pray for her mother. Then they both very excitedly began to tell me how the lady was completely healed of Pleurisy.

Of course, there's always more to the story. I was set up by God. Now, after several years of asking why I had not ever had the opportunity to reveal my Jesus to this family, many thoughts went through my mind. I had become so accustomed to in some way reaching out to these captive audiences that, in this particular set up, I could never have imagined that it would happen in this way. I'm forever grateful that God caused me to have this encounter in the most unusual way, in which I was as surprised as everyone else. I received much that day, as much as anyone else, from how He moved, revealing His love.

Chapter 10
WEATHER MIRACLES

The Rain Leaves Me Dry

The rain was coming down as I approached the Palmer fairgrounds. I knew I should have brought my raincoat, but since I didn't have it, I decided to believe that the rain would stop when I prayed or that I would not get wet. I prayed for the rain to stop only over the fairgrounds, and as I parked my truck, windshield wipers wiping the rain off the windshield, I wondered if I might have made a mistake by not bringing my raincoat.

I parked and then opened the truck door, and immediately the rain stopped. No rain was falling on the windshield—not a drop—as I got out of the truck. This was amazing, and I could hardly believe what was happening. As I walked into the fairgrounds, I was amazed to see the most unusual sight. Three hundred and sixty degrees around me, I could clearly see the rain coming down on every side, except on the fairgrounds.

I walked around the fairgrounds and prayed. And that day, people heard the gospel, many were healed, and some gave their lives to Jesus. I even stopped and guessed the weight guessers weight for fun, and I had opportunities to show people God's love and power. So many of the people I talked with had also noticed that it was raining all around, and they thought it was very unusual that it was not raining on the fairgrounds. Bless Jesus!

Rain Stops for Churchgoers

In Brazil, because of a huge storm, many of the people who were expected to attend the meeting may not have been able to get to the church, since many had to walk to get there. The team prayed all the way as we drove to the church. As the team and I filed out of the bus and into the church, our lead translator stopped me and pointed upward to show us that not only had the rain stopped, but there was a very small patch of blue sky directly over the church.

That evening, the rain stopped long enough for the people to arrive and come into the church. Once the service began, we could hear the rain pounding on the metal roof until the service was almost over, and then it stopped again. I had a very similar experience in Cali, Colombia, several years later.

Calming the Seas

While out in a boat on the ocean, on two separate occasions, I experienced some really deadly seas, and I watched them go calm in response to prayer. This happened once in Valdez, Alaska, and another time in Seward, Alaska.

Prayer for Rain Answered

In Sri Lanka, a pastor said it had not rained in his area for months. At that moment, God told me that before I left that day it would rain. I began to pray, and then I told the pastor it would rain soon. We finished lunch and then we prayed for the pastor's wife, who was being healed of carpal tunnel syndrome. As we did, the rain began.

Forest Fire Stopped

A few years ago, when a forest fire near Willow, Alaska, was out of control, a friend and I went to the edge of the fire and commanded it to stop. The next day, the local newspaper reported that the fire had stopped even though the winds were very strong. They wrote that there was no logical explanation for how the fire had stopped dead in its tracks.

Word of Knowledge in the Clouds

One day, while praying, I asked God for a new way to receive words of knowledge, and He showed me a woman's face very clearly in the clouds. As I walked down a path, I saw this lady walking toward me. I knew she was the one I had seen in the clouds, and as she approached me, I began to call out to her, telling her that the pain in her back would leave her. I stopped and talked to her, and she said she was healed as I spoke out the words. I was, at the time, on the far eastern side of an undisclosed country. Even though the community had a pastor who built all the housing in the area, including a community building with clean water, the lady I met that day—and most of the others in that area— had never heard the name of Jesus until I came to visit them.

Discovering My Authority as a Son of God

On a typical Sunday morning, in our local church, for the first time ever, the pastor's son got out from behind the sound booth and headed up to the stage. I had never heard a peep out of this young man, but when he received the microphone, he launched into a tale of being lost in the mountains of Alaska on a camping trip.

He described how, one day, the clouds had closed in on him and his father. They realized they wouldn't be able to find their way back to their camp, since they could barely see a few feet in front of them. Here's what really struck me—this young man, who was a spectator in church, reacted to the situation by commanding the clouds, "Go!"

He said that as he and his father had stood alone and stranded on the side of the mountain, they had prayed and then commanded the clouds to go. As they waited, an opening appeared in the clouds, just enough for them to see their camp. It looked like a tunnel in the clouds. They seized the opportunity to take off down the mountain, making it safely to their camp. And then, just as quickly as the clouds had opened, they closed again. *OK*, I thought to myself, *I'm in! If this guy can have authority over the weather in Jesus' name, so can I!*

This testimony caused me to begin my quest for faith to claim my God-given authority for more of my inheritance. It was there for me to claim, and at the first available opportunity, I fully planned to take hold of this gift.

At work one day, my plumbing apprentice and I had a task that would cause us to work outside in the rain all day long. When we were about to be forced off the project by the weather, I remembered the testimony of this young man and how he had commanded the clouds to go, and I decided to give it a try. Mustering up the courage, I planned to shout out, "Rain and clouds, go in Jesus' name!" Talk about doing it scared, because I was about to make a crazy statement in front of my employee, and he might think I had lost my mind. I gave it a shot anyway, even with my gospel-resistant employee looking on. I mustered up the courage to take my place as a son of God.

I walked out onto the edge of the project foundation pad and squeaked out, almost under my breath, an unanointed prayer. Then I waited for this sad little declaration to take effect while my surprised employee looked at me like bugs had just crawled out of my ears. It was still raining and blowing, and not a thing had changed. I gave it a try once again. Then, after I had repeated the command three times, a little louder each time, the weather began to improve. The rain stopped, the wind died down, and the sun peeked out of the clouds. My apprentice was now a little less resistant to the gospel. This one event caused me to press into bringing the Kingdom of heaven to other areas of my life and to gaining more faith.

During this period of time when I was believing for more authority over the weather, I was in Anchorage one day, walking into a sporting goods store with a friend, when I saw an elderly Eskimo lady approaching the truck. I immediately noticed how she was dressed in an unusually white summer parka. She was large and old, and the strangest thing was that she was hanging out with the Alaska street natives, some of whom I probably knew from ministering in Anchorage over the years.

It just didn't fit why this lady would be with them. She approached me and said, "Christian, give me 97 cents."

"What did you say?" I responded.

"Christian, give me 97 cents," she repeated.

As I tried to brush past her like this wasn't really happening, I replied, without even looking at her, "I don't have 97 cents!"

Then she said, when I was right next to her, "Christian, make the rain stop. My people have been in the rain all summer. Make the rain stop."

"You can make the rain stop yourself in Jesus' name," I replied, and I went into the store.

As I walked into the store, the fear of God came upon me. *Oh my God, I thought to myself, What have I done? That was one of God's kids, and it's not like me to react that way.*

I ran out of the store and back to the parking lot. I had only been gone for a few moments. I looked everywhere, but the woman and the people she had been with were totally gone. They had vanished. To this day, I continue to repent and ask God to never to allow me to make such a mistake again.

Chapter 11
OUT AND ABOUT

Repentance

At the fairgrounds one day, I talked with a man about Jesus while his wife visited the prophetic tent our church was manning that day. He told me that this was his wife's thing, and he really wasn't too interested in God. When he left with his wife, I really didn't think I would ever see that man again. During that same period of time, I was struggling with not seeing many people give their hearts to Jesus in the way that I had experienced previously. I always wanted to see that full-on repentance—the weeping and blubbering as the person was delivered from enslavement to darkness and addiction and completely immersed in the Holy Spirit through an encounter with God.

It's not like I never see something like that, but it's usually overseas where people respond to an altar call, like I did, and cut all their ties to the world, thus becoming, in a flash, new people. This is the kind of salvation that I was asking God for right here in the USA.

I got my wish. I was standing up front in church one Sunday morning during worship when the man I had met at the fairgrounds came up behind me and tapped me on the shoulder. What a sight he was—in his pajamas and house slippers, looking like a wreck. He told me that God woke him up and told him to come and find me. He said that he remembered the name of my church and knew he would find me and that he needed Jesus right at that moment. I told him to wait until after worship—to just wait and I would be right with him—which gave me time to think and pray about what was happening.

After worship, I took the man into a room next to the sanctuary and talked with him. He told me he had had an encounter and needed to get right with God. We prayed, and then it happened. This man just gave into the emotion that overwhelmed him in a way that I had never seen on my side of the world. There he was, bawling unrestrainedly, shaking, spluttering, and being delivered from who knows what, as he pleaded with God to forgive him for his sins. And before I even spoke another word, he was flooded with the Holy Spirit and began to speak in tongues. How amazing, astonishing, and powerful!

A Question of Perception

Recently, while sitting in my truck at a local gas pump, waiting for the tank to fill, we watched someone walk by. I asked the person I was with, "What do you see?"

The response was, "I see a woman."

I then asked, "How do you know it's a woman?"

The reply was, "I guess I don't really know."

The person I was with then asked me, "Well, what do *you* see?"

"Someone who is lost," I responded.

"How do you know they are lost?" I was asked.

"I don't know," I replied, "but I am going to assume they are lost until I find out otherwise."

My point is this—if we see God's grace or mercy as some kind of free ride or have a "wide is the way" mentality, we will see people as having their names in the book of life by some weird misinterpretation of God's love.

God, let this be my prayer: Father, please help me not to be betrayed by fear—the spirit of fear that masquerades as a false sense of wisdom or discernment that is not of you, God. Fear that tries to prevent me from reaching the lost. God help me not to be fooled by a misunderstanding of Your grace and mercy for the lost. Thank You that, by Your grace, Your power flows through us and enables us to demonstrate your salvation with healing, signs, miracles, wonders, and love to reach the lost. And thank You that for being merciful enough to equip us to set the captives free, demonstrating that Jesus is the Messiah.

Acts 4:12 says, *"Salvation is found in no one else, for there is no other name under heaven given to mankind by which we must be saved."*

And in John 3:16–18, it says:

For God so loved the world that he gave his one and only Son, that whoever believes in him shall not perish but have eternal life. For God did not send his Son into the world to condemn the world, but to save the world through him. Whoever believes in him is not condemned, but whoever does not believe stands condemned already because they have not believed in the name of God's one and only Son.

Healing at a Pastors' Meeting

At a pastors' meeting one day, I shared my testimony, preaching resurrection power and telling how the old, dead man was gone forever, forgiven. Some were healed while I shared my testimony. Others received healing as I called out words of knowledge, and some, when I asked specifically if they had a particular ailment, said they were healed at that very moment.

I had the most unusual word, and when I looked at some people in the front row, they were all blurry, like "looking through an angel" type of blurry. I felt like the woman in the group would have her vision healed, and I asked if she had poor vision. She said she did, and I said, "Be healed," and walked on, continuing to minister.

When I had those who were healed come forward, she also came up with the other pastors. Everyone was so animated—and completely healed! I felt God say that the woman who had come forward was a doctor, but I was wrong. It was her husband, sitting next to her in the front row.

As I went down the row of pastors, God gave me knowledge of each pastor, telling me their ministry titles or gifts—teacher, evangelist, street ministry, and so forth. Eventually the pastors prayed for each other. At the end of the meeting, many of the ministers actually came forward and gathered around Maria, my co-minister and translator, trying to schedule a time for us to come to their churches. Some of them were from far away cities.

Maria announced over the microphone that we had an opening the following Tuesday. I was shocked as several pastors jumped to their feet and asked us to come to their churches. They agreed instantly to meet at the largest church, and another said, "I will bring my entire church." Bless Jesus!

Snowmobile Sale Brings Salvation

While selling a couple of old snowmobiles, I met a man who came over wanting to buy both sleds. When he got out of his truck, the first thing he said was that he had cancer in the base of his spine and that he was in a lot of pain.

Immediately, without even asking his permission, I rushed over to the man and, placing my hand on his back, commanded the cancer to be gone in the name of Jesus.

The man just stood there and took it without a word, obviously not wishing to be disrespectful. I could tell he was surprised, yet he didn't want to tell me to stop.

Going through my mind at that moment was the thought that I was potentially wrecking the deal. But I didn't care if the deal fell through, as the man was going to be healed.

I watched him as he stood there, in the same place, not moving a muscle from the time that I laid hands on his back, and it seemed like he was just waiting for that moment to pass so that he could go home. When I finished praying, he thanked me sheepishly, we finalized the sale, and he went away with the old snowmobiles.

A few minutes later, I got a call from the same man saying, "The cancer at the base of my spine was the size of a baseball, and I would be in excruciating pain when I sat or drove. But now the lump is gone, and there is no pain!"

As he was telling me this, I looked out of the window to see the man walking up to my front door. We sat at the kitchen table until 1:00 am as he gave his heart to Jesus.

Saved Just in Time

Here is a story that I don't tell too often. Years ago, a man and woman from our church were constantly asking me to come and talk to their father who was an elderly man, an alcoholic, and a smoker. They were afraid that he would die not knowing Jesus. Even as they kept asking me to come and talk to the old man, I kept telling them that they should talk to him themselves. When they persistently urged me to go and speak to their father, I eventually agreed and set a time to visit with their dad.

When I went over at the time we had arranged, the man and woman met me at the front door. I asked them if their father knew I was coming, and they said he didn't. At that point, I had no strategy in place and no idea as to how I was going to handle this situation.

I went past the couple and made my way to their kitchen at the back, where I was told their father was having dinner. When I entered the kitchen, I looked to my left and saw him—a really old man seated at a small kitchen table in what was probably his underwear. He had unkempt white hair that looked like it hadn't been combed in a while and was wearing a white sleeveless t-shirt. He held a glass of vodka in his right hand and had a bottle of vodka within easy reach. A cigarette dangled from between two fingers of his left hand, and he held a fork with the remaining three, eating breakfast for dinner.

The old guy looked up at me and froze when I entered the room, and I didn't say a word as I slammed the table with my open hand. The things on the table bounced up with the impact, and I realized I had hit the table surprisingly hard and loud as well.

I looked the man in the eye and then exclaimed in a loud, stern voice, "You know why I'm here, don't you?" without actually planning on saying those words or even being aware of how they were coming out from my mouth. I don't think I was even angry, but the man looked back at me, still holding the glass full of vodka, the lit cigarette, and the fork with eggs.

He replied, "Yes, I do." He seemed neither shocked nor upset.

"It's time for you to come to know Jesus, isn't it?" I said. "God has been talking to you, hasn't He?"

"Yes, and it's time," he replied, nodding his head, still in the same frozen position.

I prayed with him as his cigarette burned away. He prayed, and you could certainly tell that he meant every word. He said that Jesus had been visiting him in his dreams and that he knew that this day would come.

I later learned that the elderly man died two weeks after this encounter. He fell in that same room where we had talked and broke his neck. I am grateful that God took me to him in time. I learned from his family that he had even begun reading the Bible. God is good!

The Veteran

While I was praying for an elderly Vietnam veteran in Palmer, Alaska, he stopped me and said, "I want to try out my new legs," and he then jumped up and walked! He walked and walked and then walked out of sight. When he came back, he thanked us, and then he said that before this the most he could walk was ten to fifteen steps. The last we saw of him, he was pushing his wheelchair away into the distance! We were more surprised than the veteran! Bless You, God!

Here's how it happened. I was walking with a couple of friends down the main street in Palmer, Alaska, after a parade. We had just watched the parade, and we were wandering along in the sunshine when we happened to see this guy sitting under a tree in his wheelchair.

It seemed a little odd, since the parade was over and almost everyone had dispersed, that this guy would still be sitting there. When I saw him, my first thought was that we have too few beautiful fourth of July summer days in this part of the world to be sitting in the shade. Yet here was this guy, missing out on the sun, so instead of just passing by, I looked at him and said hello. He was just a few feet away.

"How are you?" I asked, and we began to talk, as my young friends looked on. At some point, the man told me he had been in the wheelchair for six years, and the most he could walk was twelve steps, assisted. The next thing he knew, the three of us were around him, all praying that God would heal his body. That's when this man got up. He stood up carefully, and I truthfully didn't expect too much more than that. When he was up, he actually started walking—at first slowly, kind of hunched over. As he moved gradually forward, he began to straighten up and walk faster. And then away he went! As he was moving rapidly away from us, I was thinking, *OK, he's going to stop and come back, and say, "That's awesome!" and "Bless God!"* But no, he kept going.

He went around the corner to the right and then was gone. We were standing there where we had met him, with his abandoned wheelchair, looking at each other. I was thinking I had been duped, that there was nothing wrong with this guy, and he had somehow played us. I was wondering what I was going to say to my young apprentices. I had never had this happen before. I couldn't even figure out what had actually taken place.

Still looking at the two people with me, who were as mystified as I was, I thought, *Well, what now? Whose wheelchair is this anyway? And what just happened?*

120

I was feeling used and thinking some pretty negative thoughts about what just happened as I continued to wonder where the guy had gone off to. He'd been gone for way too long for someone who may have experienced a touch from God. Now when he had left, he had turned right and gone around a hedge where we could not see him. It was quite a distance, and none of us went after him, because we believed he was gone.

All of a sudden, this man came up from behind the spot where his wheelchair stood. He had walked all the way around this hedge lining the street, so he approached us from behind, surprising us. His face was transformed in a way that indicated he had just received an incredible miracle from God, and he was weeping uncontrollably.

He was awestruck and blessed all at the same time, and he was very receptive to the gospel. He sat back down, and we prayed with him for some time after that. It was wonderful, and I had to do some repenting secretly, because I truly had believed that I had been played by this man. The last I saw of him, he was pushing his wheelchair across the railroad tracks over to where his wife was waiting for him.

Chapter 12
EATING OUT

Salvation over Lunch

My wife and I were in Anchorage, Alaska, having lunch. As our waitress was taking our order, God began to talk to me about her situation. He began to feed me the secrets of her heart. He revealed to me that her husband was overseas in a country that I was able to name, and I even told her the sex and age of her children. I asked if I could pray for her, and as I prayed, she dropped to her knees and hung on to the edge of our table, looking down as she wept. As this was happening, I could see another waitress heading toward our table as she observed what was going on. I thought she was coming to help the other lady, but she also fell to her knees and began to cry as I prayed. Before my wife and I were done, we had two waitresses kneeling and crying at our table. It was incredible that she just joined in spontaneously.

A Waiter Hears about Jesus

While I was with friends at a restaurant in Wasilla, Alaska, God began to show me the secrets of our waiter's heart—that he had just gotten out of prison and was living with his sister to escape his old life in California. I told him that I could see a photo of him in my mind and that the picture I saw was on a wall in his mom's house. I described the type of photo and the color of the dog that was in it, and I told him that I saw that he was a professional fighter and was covered in tattoos that were concealed by his shirt. And then I told him about Jesus.

A Sudden Ministry Opportunity

I spotted two men in a restaurant one day, and walking up to them, I asked if they were pastors. I gave them a word, and they said yes, they were indeed pastors. That night I was asked to minister in their church.

Words for a Waitress

I had a word for another waitress and pointed out a ring on her wedding finger. I then asked her why, when God told me she was not married, she wore a ring on that particular finger. I then told her the age and sex of her child. I do remember that at the time she responded like none of what I said really meant anything to her. She acknowledged that it was true, but none of what I said really caused her to believe. She did say that she was interested in finding a church.

Revelations

Many times, God shows me children or loved ones of people, revealing their age, sex, and professions. He also shows me the dreams in people's hearts and what professions they want to follow.

Open Vision

Once, God showed me, in an open vision, the secrets in the heart of a waiter. I told him what his next job would be and where. I even described the restaurant that he would be working in. He said all of that was true, that he was planning to make the move soon, and that the secrets that had been revealed caused him to believe. He said he wanted to begin following Jesus, so we prayed.

A Baby Stops Crying

While at lunch with a friend one day, I noticed a baby who was crying and in agony, so I went to the mother and told her I could help. She seemed confused as I touched the child's head and the baby stopped crying. I told the mother, who said she was a Christian, that it was the power of God that had healed her baby. As I walked away, I looked back at the baby boy, and he continued to stare at me with raised hands as I walked back to my seat. Even when I sat down, the baby kept looking at me for the longest time. This was one of the many occasions when a baby has stopped crying the moment I placed my hand on him or her.

Recognition from a Child

One day, I was sitting in a restaurant alone, having a burger for lunch and minding my own business. A woman came into the restaurant with some young boys, maybe six to eight years old, and a little girl. They were all standing at the ice cream counter. I noticed one of the boys break away from the rest; he walked up very close to my table. As he turned around to go back to his friends, he blurted out, "You're a giant faith healer!" Then he just kept on walking and went back to his mom.

Holy Spirit Power

I prayed for a lady one afternoon at a restaurant, and BAM! down came the Holy Spirit. I have to admit, for the customers in the restaurant, this whole scene probably looked a bit like the lady was having a seizure. In fact, it looked exactly like a Grand Mal. As an ex-medic, I was almost convinced myself.

I noticed we were not the only ones making a commotion, and we had to ask the restaurant employees—who were running around bumping into each other and trying to decide what to do—to please not call an ambulance. Then I got a really good chance to explain to our waitress what was happening, and she actually let me pray for her also.

There is more to this story, but as I began to type it out, the Lord stopped me. He wanted this to be a private moment that should not be described with simple words that are not for a reader. This moment in time was for the woman who experienced something so holy that it could not be explained anyway, and the depth of this situation will forever belong to her and God.

Salad-Free Friday at Burger Jim's

On a recent business trip to Anchorage, the biggest city in our vicinity, my highly attuned senses began to recognize, halfway through the day, that the rumbling in my tummy was actually a ravenous hunger attacking me with a vengeance.

I had two options: I could wait until I got home, where I was assured that my beautiful wife would prepare for me any type of organically grown, non-GMO, gluten-free rabbit food that I wished for, or I could seek God's wisdom and direction as to whether I could go to lunch somewhere else. I began to ask God where I should go for lunch, and to my delight, the answer was not to await the delicacies of my wife's kitchen, but to obediently and immediately patronize the nearby gut-buster burger shop called Burger Jim's. To my delight and relief, that day had been declared Salad-Free Friday!

Not wrestling with God on His decision, I found myself speeding toward this veritable burger Mecca where the hungry can find fulfillment in meat and more meat piled high on a sesame seed bun. As I drove along, I reassured myself that God loves Burger Jim's—the place that serves everything except the food of my new lifestyle, the place where you can't, in fact, find anything green. "Well, if God wants me to have lunch there, then that is exactly what I will do," I said to myself.

As I walked toward the building, I could see homeless people all around me. Seeing them everywhere, the evangelist in me kicked in, but my stomach took precedence. Though on a mission from God, I was now sure that I was backsliding into a den of carnivorous delicacies, and I thought quickly of a strategy to restore my salvation. I began to devise a plan, my feet slipping about on the greasy entryway floor, still on a mission, but not entirely sure for whom, at that point. Then all at once a plan came to mind. I could buy lunch for someone who was already in the building.

Slipping into the sanctuary, I realized it was clearly too late to call out to the hordes of homeless and invite them into the restaurant to suffer the gut-buster of the day. My eyes were feasting on a mountain of fried meat and chemically enhanced soft drinks when, over my shoulder, I noticed a mountain of a man following me into this wonderland of delicacies. *Could this be my mission from God*, I wondered.

I asked the God of heaven, who clearly had His hand on Big Jim's wonderland, and I felt Him say, "That's the one." So there I was with this big man behind me, standing

127

at the Order Here counter, my eyes darting across the variety of meaty and cheesy choices with exuberance, having seen nothing like it for a very long while.

I quivered with obvious excitement as I didn't want to appear like a novice in this department—especially since I had at one time been a long-standing customer of such culinary delights—and I proceeded to display my knowledge of food as I requested the meat maestro behind the counter to prepare me the Super-Sized Philly Cheese Steak Burger, one of Burger Jim's Specials of the Day. All the while, of course, I kept reminding myself that this was a righteous and legitimate mission that I had been sent on by God, and there was, therefore, no guilt or shame attached to taking one for Jesus.

Taking a deep breath of the anointed surroundings, smiling with satisfaction in a dreamy sort of way, and not even trying to push back from the altar, I continued to describe the details of my order to this dealer of debauchery, even as I justified my own need of sustenance. Still clutching my wallet, I also reminded myself of my newly established holiday—Salad-Free Friday, which rendered me free of guilt as I pursued a meal free of all things green.

I finalized this proclamation by taking someone down with me, and so, before paying, I remarked politely that I would also like to purchase whatever the man behind me would like to have for his lunch. At that point, I greeted the big man behind me, noticing that he was wearing old coveralls and a hat that read Vietnam Vet. He also wore removable casts on both feet.

The man thanked me, even as he grimaced in obvious pain. I realized I was in the right place and that God loved me so much that He who gave good gifts to His kids was going to present me with a Big Jim's Special of the day and demonstrate His love by setting an army sergeant free.

All these thoughts rushed through my mind as I looked at this wounded warrior and felt justified in declaring that day Salad-Free Friday. Contemplating the growing possibilities right before me, I broke into a huge smile. *God bless Salad-Free Friday at Burger Jim's*, I thought to myself as I waited for God's glory to touch this big man and for the feast to begin.

I was so taken aback by the love of this big guy as I listened to some stories from his life. Soon he and I prayed, and then I prayed for his miracle. Thank You, Jesus, for healing Sergeant Wilbur!

Chapter 13

RANDOM MIRACLES

I had just come from a country where almost all of the conversions were due to miracles: people experiencing the power of God through a Christian. These churches were full of people who had tasted, and I fully expect this cycle to continue.

We prayed for a lady who had cancer, and she told me that all the pain was gone, and she felt really light and warm all over. I could tell she had never had an experience like that before. Another lady with broken bones in her back and constant pain was also healed. A girl gave a testimony of a terrifyingly large tumor in her breast that was now completely gone. Many others received from God.

I had a little prayer buddy, and everyone this little one touched was healed. It was truly incredible! I felt in awe of God's love. The anointing was tangible. God also gave me knowledge of details on the desires of people's hearts and their future careers. I'm so grateful to be used like this by God. Thank You, Jesus!

Sharing Gospel Power

One day, I had the privilege of sharing the gospel with someone. We sat and talked, and as I shared the story of what Jesus did for us, this person's eyes became illuminated, as if a light had been switched on.

The gospel story is so powerful. Jesus didn't come into the world to condemn it. The scripture says the world was condemned already, and that's the condition in which Jesus found it when He got here. He came to seek and save the lost. He came to set us free from death and condemnation. He offered us all eternal life, and He paid the price in full.

When this person realized the full extent of what Jesus did, he opened the door and invited Jesus in.

It's so beautiful to see what Jesus does in the life of a person who accepts His love and forgiveness. Jesus came to show us the perfect love of the Father and to demonstrate what the Kingdom of God is really like. The scripture says that when we see Jesus we see the Father.

It also tells us that Jesus on earth was the exact representation of the Father in heaven. To know Him is to love Him! To see Him is to see the Father. How can we resist such a love? Share the gospel. It is the power of God for salvation to those who believe.

One Day at the Grocery Store

Out of the blue one day, while I was in line at the grocery store, an unknown man came up to me. "Would you help me get right with God?" he asked.

I was so surprised. I was really shocked that this worried looking young man would rush up to me and begin to repent. I have to say, it took me a moment to really take in what was happening, and I don't think I responded as well as I could have. I have always looked back on this moment in time and known that something amazing happened, but I really didn't respond in the way I should have. I prayed for him for just a moment, and then I told this young man to go and get alone with God and ask Him to forgive him. That was it, and away he went.

A Cut Finger and Broken Nose

I occasionally get calls from friends who ask for prayer over the phone. One of them called one day to say he had, while at work, cut his finger to the bone with a razor knife. Before driving himself to the emergency room, he decided to stop by at his house, and when he arrived at his house, he called me to say that his finger was healed. What's more, what was once a deep gash now looked like a paper cut. He called me again the next morning to say that he was unable to tell which of his fingers had been cut.

Some months later, I got a call from the same friend who was now working in a remote place out in the bush of Alaska. He asked for prayer again, as he had suffered another accident. He had dropped a tool on the floor, and as he bent to retrieve it, he hit his nose on the rung of a ladder that he was standing next to. He went on to tell me that he must have passed out, and when he came to, he found himself on the floor in a puddle of blood. His nose was broken, and he may have suffered a concussion as well, as he was very dizzy.

So remote was the place where my friend was that he couldn't get immediate medical attention, and as he could not fly out until the following day, he was afraid even to fall asleep since there was nobody to keep an eye on him. I prayed for him and told him that I would continue to pray. The next day, he called me and told me that he had slept well and that there was no sign that he had even suffered the accident. There was no pain or bruising. Thank You, Jesus!

At the Movie Theater

After watching a movie at the local theater, my wife and I prayed for a young boy in a wheelchair inside the theater. While we prayed, the boy told me that he felt really good. I don't know if he was healed on the spot or not, but the anointing while we were praying for this boy was amazing.

Another young man came up to me after we had finished praying, and he just wanted to shake my hand. He did, and then he received a word from heaven.

At Fred Meyer

My wife and I prayed for the cashier at Fred Meyer one day. His lung problem was healed, and we felt the love of God manifest itself as we ministered to him.

At a morning meeting, God's power healed several men. Words of knowledge led to salvations and re-dedications, and then we baptized a few people because we had water and some of them wanted to seal the deal.

Precise Words of Knowledge

Have you ever had one of those precise words of knowledge for a specific person in the meeting, and you ask, "Sir, do you have pain in the upper part of your back, like a big knot?" Then he just looks at the people around him like he has no idea who you are talking to, and then you yell out, "Yes, you in the pink shirt with the grey hair!" Then he continues to look all around like it's not him you're referring to, and you hear yourself yelling, "Yes, you!"

And then you throw a sweat rag that you grab from a pastor in the front row and hit the man. And he looks and shakes his head as if to say, "No, that's not me." Meanwhile, the whole time his wife is pointing and yelling, "Yes! He complains about this all the time!"

Have you ever had that happen? I have, and the guy got healed.

More Salvations

When two young men came over at my house one day to purchase a four wheeler from me, the situation quickly, by divine appointment, escalated into salvations. Heaven is rejoicing over these men, who said they wanted what had happened to me—being adopted by a loving Father God, forgiven, and welcomed in as a friend of God, as well as a son of the most high God. Thank You, Jesus, for giving us Your Holy Spirit so a man like me can help two strangers begin their walk with You.

Lowe's

I prayed for the checkout lady at Lowe's. She likes to tell me how she doesn't go to church, but she believes. In what, I have no idea. But she always likes to hug me when I check out at her register. She says "Bless you" a lot to me, like I'm the pope or something. I found out from her months later that she really did get healed when I first prayed for her, but was afraid to say so.

Using the Gift

The doorbell on my front door rang one day, and I opened the door to a man who introduced himself and said to me, "I hear you've got a gift!"

"Yes, I do," I replied.

135

He showed me the scars on his back from all the surgeries he had undergone, and he told me about the pain he was in. We prayed, and he said the pain was gone and he could now move more freely. Then he looked at me and said, "I hear that I'm the kind of guy you used to be. Can I come back sometime and talk to you?"

Honey Elbow

I received a text from an old friend who said she was experiencing severe pain in her elbow after slipping on the ice. She asked if my wife and I could pray that God would heal her. She added that finances were tight, and she, therefore, didn't want to have to go to the hospital for x-rays. The next day, she told us she was still in pain. It had snowed the previous night, so we went to her house to see if we could help clear the snow from her driveway.

While at our friend's house, we had an opportunity to pray for her in person. We prayed a few minutes, and I began to see, in my mind, with my eyes open, what I had seen before. It was like a video playing right in front of me. I saw what I believed to be an angel—golden, like liquid honey, and very close to us, maybe even up against us, and making contact with our friend.

As we prayed, I realized I could see through the angel, and I watched it pour out a liquid of the color and consistency of honey directly onto our friend. The liquid was the same color as the angel. As this took place, I prayed that any spirit of affliction would leave. Our friend said that the pain was moving around to different places in her elbow, and the nature and intensity of the pain changed when we began to command the spirit of affliction to leave. At one point, she said the pain even got worse. From experience, I knew this was great news, as it meant that it was definitely a spirit, and we had the authority to cast it out. We continued to pray, and finally our friend said she was completely healed.

She was so animated and was jumping, laughing, and moving her arm around with a surprised look on her face as she praised God. It's such a joy when people get healed and bless God, grateful and so excited about their miracle.

Mormon Undertaker

I was called by a local business to carry out some plumbing repairs. When meeting this first-time customer, I immediately felt as if God was telling me that this man had a gift for compassion and that he cried whenever he conducted funeral services at his business. The man confirmed this, which created the opportunity for me to ask him about his relationship with God. He told me that he was Mormon. We then moved on to the plumbing repair, and I continued to talk to him about relationship and knowing God as Daddy.

I then met an employee in the next room, where I began to receive an immediate word of knowledge. I asked this young man if he had pain in his knee. He told me that he did indeed and that he had hurt his knee playing basketball. I said, "Watch this! I want to show you exactly where the pain is!" I then put my finger on the spot, and he agreed that it was the exact place. To cut a long story short, the pain went away, and I began asking him about his relationship with Jesus.

This young man told me that he also was Mormon. Later, he excitedly told his employer about being healed. *It is fun showing Jesus to people*, I thought, as we talked about miracles and raising the dead.

Chapter 14
NEW LIFE

Salvation in a Shopping Mall

I watched a young woman fall to her knees, sobbing, in the entryway of the Anchorage Fifth Avenue Mall. Dropping everything she was carrying, she crumpled into a heap on the floor. Her head dropped to the ground as she cried out loud, and I watched as someone rushed to her aid and asked if she was hurt.

At the same time as this scene was unfolding, to my left a young man slumped onto a bench near the young woman, looking distraught and defeated. His eyes never left the young woman, who was still crying, lying with her belongings that were scattered all over the floor.

I understood immediately that these two broken young people were definitely connected, and they both appeared to have hit rock bottom. In an effort to reach out, I sat down beside the young man, who looked sad, withdrawn, and exhausted. I introduced myself and shook his hand. We both looked on as the young lady was being cared for by someone who had come to her assistance.

The young man told me that his name was Charles and that the girl on the floor was his girlfriend. They were homeless, he added, and he told me he had a very painful, swollen hand from having hit someone during a fight.

I took Charles's hand and began to speak to him about the love of Jesus, and he listened, captivated. Without letting go of his hand, I continued to speak of God's love and told him how valuable he is to Him and the price He paid for those who confess their sin and believe Jesus died for them. As I spoke, he never looked away, and his eyes stayed fixed on me. All the surrounding sounds and activities slipped away into the background, as if we were the only two people in the mall. The connection I had with this young man was incredible, and his heart was truly open to the love and gospel of Jesus.

Charles told me he had run away from home because he was being abused. He told me that he had no father and that his mother's boyfriend would beat him. He explained how he had survived living on the streets for the last two years.

After we prayed, Charles examined his hand in astonishment, flexing it several times. Then he looked at me and told me that the pain was gone. On the bench that day, he asked Jesus into his heart, and I believe the powerful hand that he has on his life will set him free. I continue to believe for Charles, that he will have that new life manifest here on earth.

The Story of a Coma Bringing New Life to a Salesman

As I was driving away from our local hospital one day, heading back to work, my phone rang, and I heard a man's voice. He gave me his name. Realizing that he was a telemarketer who was going to waste a few precious moments of my time, I was about to hang up.

"Don't hang up!" the man said. "Just give me three minutes of your time. That's all I'm asking."

I considered his request for a moment before responding. "OK, I will give you the first three minutes, and then you have to give me three minutes to hear what I have to say. Are you good with that?"

He agreed and began to talk about some newly launched saw blades that would last a really long time and how he could get me a really good deal on them. I listened, and after three minutes, I asked if he was done. "Yes," he said, "and now it's your turn."

Here's what I told him: "I just left a hospital where a man I have known for several years was lying in a coma. In fact, the doctors told me that the family had notified the hospital to end treatment, as they had agreed to let him die. So I actually arrived the very day he had been unplugged from all the medical equipment that had been keeping him alive. I, and others, had been praying for this man for a few weeks, and his condition hadn't seemed to improve.

"Today, I went to the hospital and prayed again for him, not expecting much. As I walked into his room, I noticed that the television was on, and he was propped up in bed and didn't look like someone who was about to die that day. All the tubes and monitors were off except for the heart monitor. I decided to pray one last time for this man to be healed. I was alone in the room as I prayed, expecting the doctor or a family member to walk in at any moment.

"As I prayed, the man suddenly opened his eyes. It was almost like he had just awoken from a nap, and looking straight at me, he asked, 'Craig, do you know Jesus?'

"I was absolutely amazed and even confused. So many questions raced through my mind. Had he been awake for a while? Had he just come out of his coma? Whatever the answer, I just knew that this man, while in his coma, had been with Jesus.

"Stunned, I asked him if he had been awake earlier, and he said he hadn't. He didn't even ask me if he had been asleep or what had happened to him. The only question he had was, 'Do you know Jesus?'"

The salesman at the other end of the line had listened to my story in silence, and then I heard him begin to cry and confess his sins. "I want to know Jesus," he said.

"Well, the good news is that you can!" I replied, and I began to lead him in prayer. Even as I prayed with him, this telemarketer began to experience physical healing along with spiritual healing.

A month later, I got a call from him again. He just wanted to thank me, he said, for the time that I had spent talking to him the day he called to sell me saw blades. He had started going to church, he told me, and what's more, his family was going with him as well. And in answer to the question that my friend who had awakened from his coma had asked me, "Yes, I know Jesus. And He is so good!"

Shields Up

As soon as I entered her home, my customer and I began to make small talk as I evaluated the problem with her garage heater. "Yes, you were right to call me, because the heater is definitely leaking water and needs to be repaired," I said.

I returned to my truck to get more tools and the necessary parts for the repair, and I got started repairing the leaky garage heater.

We continued to talk as I worked, and I told her about the home I had for sale; mine had been on the market for quite a while, and I told her I hoped hers sold faster. We kept talking as I worked, and then she asked me a simple question about the home I had for sale. I answered her question and then launched into a testimony of Jesus and how God had given us a new home.

"It sounds like God really does do things like that, even today," she said. "I wish I could hear from God like they used to in biblical times."

About that time, I got a sharp pain in my stomach, and I knew this was not my pain, or at least I hoped it wasn't. I found myself devising a way to make good on this word from the Lord.

"You can hear from God like they did back then," I told her. "Actually, for people these days who are in a relationship with Jesus, this sort of thing is expected. God shows us how we can hear His voice, and He demonstrates His love for people," I said. "For example, sometimes God will, in His own way, tell me that someone around me has pain in their stomach, and then I will have an opportunity to ask, pray, and believe that God will heal that person."

Then I finally asked her, "Do you have a pain in your stomach?"

"You do hear from God," she replied. "I have Crohn's disease."

I said, "Let's pray!" and the pain immediately left.

The pain was gone—the very pain that had caused her to come home sick from work.

When it comes to words of knowledge, I don't know if anyone has gotten mad at me for asking if they had pain, but if the situation was awkward, it was usually because of something I brought into it. Sometimes I'm the one bringing all the fear into the situation, and I'm the one who is preparing for rejection. The realization that you are right where you're supposed to be for such a precise mission isn't always on the front burner. We're not usually ready for a divine appointment and don't expect a favorable reply.

I size up the afflicted like they are my competition, and I come to conclusions about whether God does or doesn't want to heal a particular person. Or maybe I feel that they have more unbelief than I have faith, so I won't ask to pray. Maybe, I think, they are set to reject me the instant I speak the name of the Lord.

Maybe these folks are desperately seeking God, and they just don't know it. Many times, people are positioned by God for this very exchange, and we go into this like we're running into a ring with a dangerous bull—without a plan or protection. Faith is in part the willingness to take the first step, to run into the ring, believing you are on point, that you are exactly where you're destined by God to be for that exact moment in time, and that you are equipped.

It's in the second step toward your imagined doom that God meets you, and the Holy Spirit gives you the words to say. This may happen just an hour or minutes before or even as you speak. Maybe you have nothing, it's a complete miss, and your word of knowledge hits the floor like a stone. But then you hear something like this from your divine appointment: "No, I don't have pain in my ear. Why do you ask me that?"

Now you have several options. First, this person may have lied. People sometimes do people things. You have no idea this is happening, but this person is internally dealing with your question, which was spot on, and inside he or she is screaming, "There really is a God, and this God just told you a secret nobody knew!" So, even though you don't know what is happening, something is definitely happening in that person. You just need to trust God with the results.

Second, this person doesn't have pain where you indicated, but maybe the pain is somewhere else. Game on! Or, the person has no pain at all, but is curious about why you asked. This is an opportunity for the gospel.

Deliverance Mode

If you are fortunate enough to be my pre-Christian customer and you are planning to look over my shoulder or hang out in the same room with me while I work, you're going to hear my testimony, and I'm going to preach the gospel while I work. Period.

As I backed into a customer's driveway, I saw in my truck mirrors that his yard was decorated with various shrines and other unusual miscellaneous artifacts—evidence of a misunderstanding of who God really is. Getting out of the truck, I could clearly see more of this man's collection of every goofy shrine and idol imaginable. I almost began to think this guy was just kidding with all this junk and was just having fun with his weird collection of idols.

Entering his home, I realize that he was, in fact, someone who thinks he should cover every religious base and believe in all the "gods." I learned that he was of Indian origin, though American born, as we talked and headed down the narrow stairs to the poorly lit basement.

He showed me the boiler for heating his home, and we talked about what could be wrong with it. Once I diagnosed the problem, I began to carry out the repair. Then I realized that this guy wanted to hang out with me. I immediately and fearlessly started telling him about my Jesus. I was telling Jesus stories like I had a death wish, just hammering away on the reality of who God is and the power of His Son's resurrection. I was starting to think that I was, in reality, looking for trouble. Maybe I was intentionally starting a fight with the macabre collection of voodoo items, and if I played my cards right, I might cause something to break and loose the spirit (as this has happened in the past). So now I was counting on it. I continued to talk about the radical love of Jesus as I worked. Maybe I went a little over the top, but I would much rather tell Jesus stories than work on nasty old boilers anyway.

I was bent over, removing an old boiler water pump, while the customer looked over my shoulder just inches behind me. Boldly, I told him all about the life of Jesus while working away, having the time of my life. I was pretty aware that this guy was nearly on top of me holding up a work light. Because he didn't smell bad, I was kind of OK with him being my helper. Looking over my shoulder, I could see that this man had the wildest look on his face—big eyes and everything. I thought to myself, *Have I hit all the right buttons? Is this guy going to full-on manifest? Is he going to be delivered?* This guy had all the markings for a critter fest!

Hair standing straight up on the back of my neck, I looked at the man again. He was still grinning from ear to ear, his eyes as big as silver dollars. I was thinking, *OK, here we go. This is about to get really crazy.* So I ramped up the Jesus stories, going for the grand finale. I almost had the pump apart when I started hearing the strangest thing—this guy was growling, a real-deal, scary type of growling with guttural sounds, like a six-thousand-year-old demon from the pit itself sort of growl. I looked back again at the home owner, who was inches behind me. All I could see was a huge smile, like he had not heard a sound. Fully aware of the sound, I quickly deployed emergency tongs.

I looked back at the pump, and I heard the growl again exactly the same as before. The hair on my neck was now at full attention, and I realized I was still speaking about the goodness of God, but in an almost manic way, so as to spur the demonic toward the main event.

I looked at the man again, expecting to be attacked by this seventy-five-year-old shrunken savage, but he was still just smiling that same devious smile. This time, the look on his face said, "I'm partnering with devils."

I was done preaching. Expecting armed gargoyles to rush down the stairs, I was in full-on combat, self-defense, and deliverance mode. And it happened again. *Dang!* As I turned and leaped to my feet, I noticed something halfway into my spin, with pipe wrench in hand. It was still a blur, yet out of the corner of my eye I was processing brand new information while almost crashing into Fred-of-the-living-dead. I watched this seemingly possessed tiny man trying to keep his balance while quickly backing up to get out of my way, still with his flashlight in hand. He was extremely surprised and possibly innocent.

It was then that I realized that the devilish sound I was hearing was actually coming from water running backwards through the piping connected to the old boiler pump and draining on to the floor. *Gurrrrr Gurr rup rup.*

ABOUT THE AUTHOR

My name is Craig Pearcy. I was born in Anchorage, Alaska. I met Ruth Vinson, my now wife, on New Year's Eve 1985 in Valdez, Alaska. We married in June of 1986 and then traveled around the United States for several years as I worked construction as a heavy equipment operator.

I believed and was born again right after reading a book about heaven and hell in Pasco, Washington, on September 13, 1992. That same month, we then traveled back to Alaska and settled down, building a home in the small town of Wasilla.

Our two children were born in 1997 and 1999. Our family soon landed in a local church, growing closer to Jesus. In 2007, as we were able, Ruth and I began to go on mission trips with Global Awaking to Brazil. This is where we met Bill Dew of Dewnamis Ministries, and I began to go on mission trips as often as I could just to be in the purposes of Jesus (the anointing) and gather all the experience I could. I simply loved seeing people's lives change radically by encounters with Jesus, and I loved learning to represent Jesus Christ.

Encouraged by Bill Dew and others, my wife Ruth and I began Paragon Global Inc in 2010 :

contact pearcy@mtaonline.net

I continued to minister *as I go* at home in Alaska. I also continued to travel with Bill occasionally, and gradually I began to take teams on my own to various countries around the world, doing my part to equip the teams and receiving impartations from those we would minister with and to.

In January of 2019, Ruth and I made another leap of faith and sold our plumbing and healing business of almost twenty years. From that point, we spent the next nine months at a YWAM base in Kona, Hawaii, discipling several young mission builders and YWAM students in the *as you go* life style. All of these young men and women continue to walk with Jesus, and many are now purposely and intentionally discipling others by example. They preach the gospel, heal the sick, cast out demons, and repeat.

HODOS PUBLISHING

▌ GOD'S BARAK – Alain Caron

▌ APOSTOLIC CENTERS – Alain Caron

▌ APOSTOLIC CENTERS – WORKBOOK – Alain Caron

▌ HEAVEN'S HEADQUARTERS – Alain Caron

▌ BRINGING BACK THE GLORY – Alain Caron

▌ APOSTOLIC EXPANSION – Alain Caron

▌ THE GLORY OF THE SECRET PLACE – Alain Caron

▌ STIRRED BY A NOBLE THEME – Annie Elliott

Distribution Canada: **hodos.ca**

Hodos Apostolic Network
480 Vernon, Gatineau, QC
CANADA J9J 3K5
+1 (613) 791-8552
hodos.ca

Made in the USA
Las Vegas, NV
19 January 2022

41824501R00090